Promising Practices Connecting Schools to Families of Children with Special Needs

A Volume in
Family School Community Partnership Issues

Promising Practices Connecting Schools to Families of Children with Special Needs

Edited by

Diana B. Hiatt-Michael
Pepperdine University

INFORMATION AGE
PUBLISHING

80 Mason Street
Greenwich, Connecticut 06830

Library of Congress Cataloging-in-Publication Data

Promising practices connecting schools to families of children with
special needs / edited by Diana B. Hiatt-Michael.
    p. cm. – (Family, school, community, partnership)
Includes bibliographical references (p.   ) and index.
  ISBN 1-930608-98-5 (pbk.) – ISBN 1-930608-99-3 (hardcover)
  1. Children with disabilities–Education–United States. 2. Special
education–Parent participation–United States. 3. Home and
school–United States. 4. Community and school–United States. I.
Hiatt-Michael, Diana B. II. Series.
  .LC4031.P76 2004
  371.9'0973–dc22

                                    2003024766

Copyright © 2004 Information Age Publishing, Inc.

Printed in the United States of America

CONTENTS

DEDICATION

This monograph was lovingly prepared by the authors and dedicated to all the families of children with special needs and the teachers who enrich their lives. In particular, the editor dedicates her work to her granddaughter, Rachel Marie Hiatt.

ACKNOWLEDGEMENTS

As Editor of the Family School Community Partnership Special Interest Group's monograph, I extend my appreciation to the Executive Board of this American Education Research Association Special Interest Group and Ollie Moles, who serve as the editorial board for this series. Their advice, critiques, and support bring together the best scholars to contribute their wisdom to this monograph. The editorial board for this monograph includes the following:

- Diana B. Hiatt-Michael, Series Editor
- Oliver Moles, Consultant, Rockville, MD
- Lee Shumow, Associate Professor, Educational Psychology and Foundations, Northern Illinois University
- Howard Kirschenbaum, Frontier Professor of School, Family, and Community Relations and Chair, Counseling and Human Development Program at University of Rochester
- Mary M. Cornish, Associate Professor, Plymouth University
- Pat Hulsebosch, Professor, Department of Education, Gallaudet University
- Brent McBride, Professor of Education, University of Illinois-Champaign
- Mary Ann Burke, Program Analyst for the Santa Clara Valley Health & Hospital System Department of Alcohol & Drug Services, Campbell, CA; Adjunct Lecturer, California State University
- Karen Mapp, President, Institute for Responsive Education, and Adjunct Professor, Northeastern University

I am grateful to the dedicated scholars who contributed chapters to this monograph. Each person has a particular expertise and brought the best of their experience and thought to their chapter. You serve as an inspiration to everyone in this Special Interest Group. Their names are listed under Contributors. It was my honor to dialogue with each one and follow their thinking as each chapter emerged to its published state.

My appreciation is extended to my colleagues and friends, Associate Dean Bob Paull, Dean Margaret Weber, Provost Darryl Tippens, and President Andrew Benton who embrace scholarship endeavors at Pepperdine University and whose support made this volume possible. I am deeply indebted to my husband John for his understanding, keen insights, and probing questions. A special note of recognition is presented to Ardell Broadbent, Janet Cosman-Ross and Patrick Ross for their thoughtful editing. During the final process, various editorial board members and practitioners read chapters and provided insightful suggestions. Special thanks to these scholars and practitioners—Paul Amuchi, Juanita Coleman-Merritt, Mary Cornish, Melinda Docter, Scott Gray, Laura Hiatt, Oliver Moles, Patrick and Janet Ross, Sissy Sandeen, and Lee Shumow.

Diana B. Hiatt-Michael
Professor of Education
Pepperdine University

LIST OF CONTRIBUTORS

Rosalyn Anstine-Templeton

Associate Dean, College of Education and Human Services, Ferris State University, Big Rapids, MI

Margie Buttignol

Teacher and Independent Scholar, Toronto Catholic District School Board/North York General Hospital, Toronto, Ontario, Canada

Carl I. Fertman

Associate Professor, School of Education, University of Pittsburgh, PA

Diana B. Hiatt-Michael

Professor of Education, Graduate School of Education and Psychology, Pepperdine University, West Los Angeles, CA

Pat Hulsebosch

Professor of Education, Gallaudet University, Washington, DC

Belinda D. Karge

Professor and Special Education Department Chair, California State University—Fullerton, CA

Michelle A. Johnston

Dean, College of Education and Human Services, Ferris State University, Big Rapids, MI

Hwa Lee

Assistant Professor, Bradley University, Peoria, IL

Shawna Lightbody

Clinical Psychologist, North York General Hospital, Toronto, Canada

Lynda R. Myers   Social Worker, Jewish Social Service Agency of
                                    Metropolitan Washington DC

Lynn A. Newman   Senior Education Researcher, SRI
                                    International, Menlo Park, CA

Michaelene M. Ostrosky   Associate Professor in Special Education,
                                    University of Illinois-Urbana-Champaign, IL

Leland L. Simmons   Speech-Language Pathologist, Pomona
                                    Unified School District, CA

Leigh Solomon   Child and Adolescent Psychiatrist,
                                    Psychiatrist/Clinical Director, North York
                                    General Hospital, Toronto, Canada

Cheryl Williams   Coordinator/Clinical Nurse Specialist, Child
                                    and Mental Health Unit, North York General
                                    Hospital, Toronto, Canada

FOREWARD

Diana B. Hiatt-Michael

This is the third in a series of monographs by the Family, School, Community Partnership Special Interest Group of the American Educational Research Association. This monograph focuses on an important subgroup of parents and children, those with special needs, and reveals an emerging positive portrait connecting these families within the mainstream of the community and public education. The authors in this volume raise significant educational issues from the perspectives of classroom teachers, other educators, researchers, and parents of children with special needs.

This third monograph follows the first two volumes in the series that include *Promising Practices In Family Involvement in Schools* and *Promising Practices to Connect Schools with the Community*. These three volumes are a comprehensive resource connecting the most outstanding practices supported by research.

Parent involvement, as one of the eight National Education Goals in 1994, has brought heightened awareness to the importance of connecting educational institutions and their communities. The goal envisions "school partnerships that will increase parent involvement and participation in promoting the social, emotional, and academic growth of children." The U.S. Congress additionally supported this goal in the passage of the *No Child Left Behind Act* in 2001. This act is the renewal of the Elementary and

Promising Practices Connecting Schools to Families of Children with Special Needs, pages xiii–xv.
A Volume in: Family School Community Partnership Issues
Copyright © 2004 by Information Age Publishing, Inc.
ISBN: 1-930608-99-3 (hardcover), 1-930608-98-5 (paperback)

Secondary Education Act and strongly promotes schools' active involvement with families and the surrounding community. The federal legislation PL 105-17 Individuals with Disabilities Education Act [IDEA] 1997 augmented the role of parents of children with special needs, initially mandated by the Education for all Handicapped Children Act PL 94-142. This monograph reflects the thrust of the federal direction created by the IDEA 1997 and its current re-authorization.

The purpose of this series is to provide practitioners and researchers a forum for securing the most current knowledge pertinent to family, school, and community partnership issues. Family, school, and community partnerships involve persons across educational and relational groups, including administrators, students, community groups, teacher training institutions, policymakers, businesses, as well as parents and other family members.

This series sponsors a monograph on an annual or biennial basis and will focus on selected themes for each issue. Each monograph will highlight the most comprehensive and robust theory and practice. The Executive Board and membership of the Family, School, Community Partnership Special Interest Group [SIG] of the American Educational Research Association [AERA] serves as the sponsor of this series. This group determines the themes and topics for each monograph.

The series Editorial Board serves as the directors and producers of each monograph. As the editorial board discussed the topic and possible chapters for this year's monograph, we concluded that not every IDEA disability group, namely thirteen federal categories, could be specifically assigned a chapter. The monograph would have burgeoned to a tome. We provided an open proposal to all members of our SIG, AERA members, and educators in special education. A large number of individuals who did research on or directed model programs for children with special needs responded. The editor dialogued with these respondents, describing the SIG's requirements for a focus on promising practices in family-school-community involvement supported by research. Several promising authors provided outlines or completed articles in response to our call and these discussions. The editorial board individually reviewed these prospective chapters and determined, by consensus, which chapters held promise for this particular monograph. The editor assumed responsibility to nurture these authors, provide deadlines, suggest revisions and edits, and applaud the final product. The editorial board served as readers for each chapter and suggested appropriate revisions.

The first four chapters provide the reader with overviews of the monograph's major themes. This first chapter by the editor, a former primary-grade teacher and later the director/teacher of a four-year private practice with learning disabled children, provides the background and framework for family involvement in issues related to children with special needs. The second chapter by Simmons, a doctoral candidate whose dissertation deals with family-school involvement, offers the historical and legal actions taken by parents of children with special needs. In addition, he provides information related to inclusion, the placement of children with special needs in the general education classroom. The third chapter presents the findings of a ground-breaking nationwide SRI study completed in 2003 under the direction of Newman. Her data analysis reveals the degree and ways families of children with special needs are actively involved in their children's education. The fourth chapter by Karge, an author highly regarded by special education teachers, discusses adapting the curriculum across the lifespan for children with special needs. This chapter illustrates numerous avenues that parents and schools should travel together so that children with special needs may reach academic success in the classroom.

The next group of five chapters focus on selected categories of children with special needs. Anstine-Templeton and Johnson provide powerful insights to promising practices for the largest group of children with special needs, those with learning disabilities. More than one out of two children with special needs are primarily categorized as learning disabled. Her chapter describes the major types of learning disabilities, their characteristics, prevalence, and ways to support academic and social success at home and school. Fertman, a dedicated researcher and professor regarding families and children with behavioral disorders, deals with families whose children are diagnosed as emotionally disturbed, and shares the challenges of these children to both the families and the school. Lee, also a mother of a talented deaf child, and Ostrosky share keen insights into families with developmentally delayed children and their perceptions of school staff. Her independent activities include working with the construction of adaptive toys and devices for these children. Hulsebosch, professor at Gallaudet College, a leader in education for the deaf, and Myers, a social worker with the Jewish Social Service Agency of Greater Washington DC, team to offer their wisdom for work with deaf children and their families. Lastly, Buttignol and associates at Toronto's North York General Hospital describe an innovative hospital-based classroom for children with special needs sponsored by the Ontario Ministry of Health .

Please advise us regarding the worth and use of this monograph to you and others. The series editor may be reached at dmichael@pepperdine.edu.

CHAPTER 1

CONNECTING SCHOOLS TO FAMILIES OF CHILDREN WITH SPECIAL NEEDS

Diana B. Hiatt-Michael

A CHANGING LANDSCAPE

Special education has been a rapidly changing field during the past 50 years. Families of children with special needs played a critical advocacy role in this change. The story has been one of passionate commitment from parents and special education leaders to promote change from segregated living to segregated education and ultimately to inclusion in mainstream education. Initially, these changes were fueled by increasing social consciousness that the U.S. Constitution calls for the equality of all citizens. This change in social consciousness led to legal action, first in courts and then in the federal legislature. Prior to the passage of the Education for All Handicapped Children Act in 1975, one million children with disabilities were not in public schools, and 90 percent of children with diagnosed developmental disabilities were maintained in state-operated institutions (Tollestrup, 2003, p. 16). In response to the strong and continued advocacy of equal opportunity for individuals with disabilities, President George

Promising Practices Connecting Schools to Families of Children with Special Needs, pages 1–14.
A Volume in: Family School Community Partnership Issues
Copyright © 2004 by Information Age Publishing, Inc.
All rights of reproduction in any form reserved.
ISBN: 1-930608-99-3 (hardcover), 1-930608-98-5 (paperback)

W. Bush (2001) remarked at the New Freedom Initiative that "Old misconceptions about physical and mental disability are being discredited. . . . We must speed up the day when the last barrier has been removed to full and independent lives for every American with or without a disability" (para. 7).

The slogan "Who says I can't?" rallies families and children with special needs to strive for equality and independent action (Hales, 2003). Parents of children with special needs continue to be at the forefront of legal battles to provide appropriate educational services, support, and opportunities. In addition to legal action, parents and schools have joined together to utilize technological advances in equipment, computer devices, instructional strategies, and medicine. The chapters of this monograph highlight the role of parents of children with special needs and the role of the school. Parents act as the primary source of knowledge and home support for their children, and the school provides the educational expertise, support, and resources for these children and their families.

SNAPSHOT OF A CLASSROOM
PRIOR TO FEDERAL LEGISLATION

When I began teaching in 1960, the concept of special education classes located within public school sites was voluntarily being implemented by forward-looking school districts. For that era, public-supported special education was an innovation. Prior to the late 1950s, moderately and severely disabled children were not in public schools but kept at home, in private settings, or in state institutions. At my newly opened elementary school in West Hartford, Connecticut, the school district established two classes for developmentally delayed children of primary school age, one termed *mentally retarded* and the other *emotionally disturbed,* and a third class for children with *physically handicapping* conditions. Teachers with or without special certification instructed these classes. These teachers taught the children on a whole group basis because an Individualized Educational Program (IEP) as mandated after the 1975 law was not required. At this time, children who would now be diagnosed with learning disabilities—and who presently number half of the children with special needs—were not diagnosed. These children did not receive special services and were included in all general education classrooms.

The mainstreaming of children in these segregated special education classrooms only occurred as an informal arrangement between the special education teacher and a general education classroom teacher. Another teacher and I, the only 2 among the 25 faculty members at the school, opened our doors for these disabled students to participate in class activities. Special education teachers cautiously brought selected children to visit for short periods. Initial activities included music, art, literature, and science. These children could watch or participate as they chose. However, like most teacher-based innovations, this rudimentary degree of main-streaming ended when we left the school. Thus, it was imperative that to further connect families of children with special needs to the school, parents continue to advocate for legislation to mainstream their children.

AN ERA OF PARENT ADVOCATED FEDERAL LEGAL CHANGES

Various court decisions during the 1950s and 1960s, described in Chapter 2 led to ground-breaking federal legislation, first the Handicapped Children's Early Education Assistance Act, P.L. 90-538 in 1968, and later the Education for All Handicapped Children Act, P.L. 94-142 in 1975. These acts supported the integration of children with special needs living outside the mainstream of the school community into the public schools, namely children living in their family's home or in a full-care institution. P.L. 94-142 mandated financial support within the public school system for all types of children with special needs. This act was the basis for a subsequent fervor of educational activities, including teacher preparation programs for special education, development of classrooms for special education, and provisions for services within each school district. The National Center of Educational Statistics (2001) reports sizeable growth for education funding between 1965 and 1975. Individualized instruction, an innovative concept in the 1950s and 1960s, but one that almost disappeared in general education classrooms during the 1980s, served as the basis for the IEP that continues in special education today (Hiatt, 1971, pp.28-29).

In spite of this earlier progress, NCES (2001) reveals a "substantial" decrease in educational funding during the 1980s. This decade marked a return to the core curriculum with a new focus on standards and testing. Special education programs received less public education attention, and special education funds often served to meet general school needs. Parents became concerned that these hard-won monies for children with special needs were stretched to serve normal children. They also noted any school policies that altered their conception of P.L. 94-142. Parent advocate groups lobbied for additional legislation to protect their children's rights. The Association for Retarded Citizens and the Association for Children and Adults with Disabilities coordinated efforts with the various associations serving differing types of disabilities in this drive for enforcement of P. L. 94-142. They received encouragement from the federal government through the passage of the Handicapped Children's Protective Act of 1986, P.L. 99-372. This act permitted parents of children with special needs to collect attorneys' fees in cases brought under the Education for All Handicapped Children Act. P.L. 99-372 served as the foundation for parents' financial capability to advocate for appropriate changes in education policy and procedures.

Parents' insistent and persistent pressures, coupled with support of special education leaders, led to passage of various acts and the current Individuals with Disabilities Education Amendments Act (IDEA) of 1997. IDEA describes the Least Restrictive Environment:

> IN GENERAL—To the extent appropriate, children with disabilities, including children in public and private institutions or other care facilities, are educated with children who are not disabled, and special classes, separate schooling, or other removal of children with disabilities from the regular educational environment occurs only when the nature or severity of the disability of the child is such that education in regular classes with the use of supplementary aids and services cannot be achieved satisfactorily. (Section 612.5, Office of Special Education and Rehabilitative Services, 2003, p.30)

In conjunction with each change, the use of language to describe these children was revised.

THE CURRENT LEGISLATIVE BASIS OF
FAMILY INVOLVEMENT IN SCHOOLS

IDEA 1997 extends parental involvement and provides the vision of seamless interagency services for families of children with special needs. Section 614 of IDEA states that parents are to be part and parcel of the design, evaluation, and where appropriate implementation of school-based improvement plans. In addition, the act provides for parent training, information centers and activities, and timely technical assistance (Section 681). The act provides for funds that "shall be used to pay the excess costs of providing special education and related services to children with disabilities" (Section 613.2; Office of Special Education and Rehabilitative Services, 2003, p. 42). This act expressly prohibits the commingling of federal funds paid to a state for children with special needs and related services with other state funds.

Children with special needs aged 3 through 21 number over 6,500,000 in the U.S. and account for about 10 percent of K-12 public school children (National Center for Education Statistics, 2001; Paige, 2003). Although states are the primary source of general education funds, the federal government serves a major role in funding programs for persons with disabilities. The Department of Education is the source for about 40 percent of federal funding in special education, but many other departments such as the Department of Health and Human Services, Department of Labor, Department of the Interior, National Science Foundation, and other federal agencies fund educational services for families of children with special needs (National Center for Educational Statistics, 2001).

IDEA 1997 rests on 20 years of research and encourages utilization of this research. IDEA recommends for effective education of children with disabilities the following:

A. having high expectations for such children and ensuring their access in the general curriculum to the maximum extent possible;

B. strengthening the role of parents and ensuring that families of such children have meaningful opportunities to participate in the education of their children at school and at home;

C. coordinating this act with other local, educational service agency, state, and federal school improvement efforts in order to ensure that such children benefit from such efforts and that special education can become a service for such children rather than a place where they are sent;

D. providing appropriate special education and related services and aids and supports in the regular classroom to such children, whenever appropriate;

E. supporting high-quality, intensive professional development for all personnel who work with such children in order to ensure that they have the skills and knowledge necessary to enable them—

   a. to meet developmental goals and, to the maximum extent possible, those challenging expectations that have been established for all children; and

   b. to be prepared to lead productive, independent, adult lives, to the maximum extent possible (Office of Special Education and Rehabilitative Services, 2003, pp.5-6).

IDEA strengthens the basic rights of children with special needs both through:

A. the right to a free appropriate public education . . . for all children with disabilities, including children suspended or expelled from school; and

B. the procedural safeguards for these children and their parents (Office of Special Education and Rehabilitative Services, 2003, p. 8).

IDEA emphasizes that children with disabilities "have meaningful access to the general education through improvement to the IEP, and are included in general education reform efforts related to accountability and high expectations, and that focus on improved teaching and learning" (Office of Special Education Programs, 1999).

When P.L. 94-142 opened the school doors to all children with disabilities in 1975, parents and teachers of general education students expressed reservations about the effect some of these children, especially those with emotional disorders, might have upon academic achievement of other children. Public school administrators and teachers are responsible for the care of all children, not just focusing on the unique needs of children with disabilities. In response to such concerns, IDEA has developed a large section in the procedures on discipline for children with disabilities (Office of Special Education and Rehabilitative Services, 2003). The regulations do not permit suspension simply because the teachers cannot work with the child, but there are safeguards for appropriate suspension, expulsion, and behavior assessment to protect the rights of all children and school personnel. Children with disabilities must adhere to regulations regarding weapons at school and use of illegal drugs. School personnel must also balance the educational needs of the total class with the special needs of a given child.

THE ISSUES OF INCLUSION

The appropriate degree of mainstreaming and inclusion is a source of continuing debate. The authors in this monograph support the concept of the inclusion of children with special needs into general education classes but only as appropriate for each individual and their families. As noted by Simmons in Chapter 2 and every other author in this monograph, inclusion does not mean an elimination of full-day or resource-type special education classes. The type and amount of time spent in various educational settings will be determined by the IEP developed among families, school staff, and various support personnel (Section 614). Parents assume the prominent role in the development of the IEP. An IEP reflects available services and personnel as well as parental preferences for any given child with special needs. Charter schools and private schools that educate children with special needs may receive funds if they adhere to the policies in IDEA.

Inclusion in general education benefits both special education and general education students (J. Coleman-Merritt, J. Fabrocini, B. Karge, H. Lee, & L. Simmons, personal communications, July 2003). The general education students become tolerant and accepting of children with special needs; they become aware of the limitations and gifts of each person. The children with special needs acquire knowledge and skills to live in the community, understand various types of children, and become more independent. Byrnes (2003), parent of a child with multiple disabilities, asserts that "his placement in a general education classroom with additional supports and services has given him a gateway into the broader community (p. 7)." General education teachers benefit from the added assistance of other adults who are assigned as aides to the classroom. Student/adult ratio is lowered in a cost-effective manner (Hiatt & Keesling, 1980). A special bonus is that there are increased support specialists such as family counselors, speech pathologists, occupational therapists, physical therapists, and psychologists available to general education school sites. An itinerant inclusion facilitator for Los Angeles Unified School District remarked that some IEP teams may include up to 26 service providers (M. Docter, personal communication, July 30, 2003).

Interviews by the author with special education facilitators emphasized the importance that all parties agree on and accept the given provisions of any IEP. The federally-funded national study reported in Chapter 3 reveals a high degree of parent involvement in IEP team meetings. The degree and kind of inclusion is unique to each situation. For example, if the parents feel that more time in a special day-class will benefit their child, but the teachers and support specialists suggest more time within the general education classroom, the child will hear disparate messages. The degree of satisfaction with IEP implementation is based upon a consensus that is within the tolerance level of all parties. Comments and examples by various authors in this monograph expand upon the importance of this consensus.

TECHNOLOGY AND MEDICAL ADVANCES SUPPORT FAMILY-SCHOOL CONNECTIONS

Technology has provided the tools to assist children with special needs to be more independent at school and home and to more easily enter the mainstream action of the school and community. Such advances encourage independence. Wheelchairs are adapted to support the mobility of each physically handicapped child. Computerized technology assist disabled children in mobility, speech, hearing, and adaptive learning. Speech synthesizers coupled with text-to-speech systems, touch screen devices, and voice output communication aids are a few of the many technological aides that support independence of children with handicapping conditions in the general education classroom. For children with visual impairments, voice recognition systems and refreshable Braille displays offer the capability to read independently. Educators can create CDs and videos to encourage vocabulary building and language use for children with delayed language development, pervasive developmental disorders, and autism. Switches are an increasingly popular device to adapt educational materials and popular toys for children with mobility limitations (Adaptive Technology Resource Centre, n.d.).

In addition to electronic technology, instructional techniques and strategies have been developed to equip families and their children with special needs with better learning tools. Classroom techniques such as those described in chapters 4, 5, 6, and 8 are powerful methods for families and teachers to join hands and educate children with special needs. For example, in some schools parents, teachers, and other members of the IEP team are encouraged to utilize a Student Environment Test Tool (SETT) to analyze the school environment (Zabala, 1996). Based upon this assessment, parents work with teachers to provide appropriate accommodations and adaptations for the child. The open classroom approach reintroduced peer teaching and cross-age teaching, opportunities to bring together general education students with those with special needs. Johnson, Johnson, and Holubec's (1994) cooperative learning approaches provide an instructional strategy so that children with special needs collaborative with general education students at the same work table in the classroom.

New knowledge has altered public conceptions of learning methods of all children as well as those classified with disabilities. Education concepts such as Armstrong's (1994) application of Gardner's multiple intelligences for the general classroom and Tomlinson's (1999) differentiated instruction, have influenced parents' and teachers' conception of the uniqueness of each child. In addition, Levine (2002), a professor of pediatrics, promotes the uniqueness of every person's mind and the way it operates. He connects emerging knowledge of the brain's physiology with children's learning capabilities. He encourages parents and teachers to analyze content to be acquired and determine the most effective way to instruct a given child. He discourages teaching as "one size fits all."

Throughout the country various centers have developed structured approaches to education and provided training for parents and classroom teachers. IDEA supports training of school personnel and parents. In California, the Department of Education's Diagnostic Center sponsored state-wide training to address school-wide behavior supports, discipline, behavior support plans, and classroom strategies (California Department of Education, n.d.). Across the nation, every state has one to several parent intervention centers. These centers provide information, serve as networks of interagency services, and offer ways that families can connect to the school and effectively parent their child with special needs. For example, a California center provides "Homework Support Through Technology." This program is free and utilizes help with and without computers. In addition, the program offers technology solutions, such as screen readers, talking word processors, and adapted keyboards. Medical centers, such as the Neuropsychiatric Institute at UCLA, offer instructional programs to connect parents and teachers with advances in educational techniques for children with mental and emotional disabilities. Brunstrom, a pediatrician specializing in neurology who has cerebral palsy, adapted martial arts for children with cerebral palsy (Hales, 2003). At the school site, the development of resource rooms for support personnel or pull-out programs offer a place where parents, teachers, students, and specialized staff may join together to work with children with similar problems. For example, resource rooms may be utilized for children with attention deficit disorder and those with emotional disorders who focus more effectively with fewer distractions. These special spaces or classrooms with fewer children can provide the most appropriate environment for learning.

Medical and genetic research has dramatically opened a range of options for children with special needs. New drugs, methods of injection and doses, and surgeries to redesign the physical abnormalities provide ways to help children with disabilities. These children have options to control their behavior and assume a greater independence from the underlying disability. Children with cerebral palsy may select injections to temporarily relax muscles or another medicine that can be administered by a pump into the spinal fluid to relax stiff muscles. The Mayo Clinic website on Attention Deficit Hyperactive Disorder (ADHD) describes a child who takes "his thinking pill"(Mayo Foundation for Medical Education and Research, 2003). Chapter 5 focuses on the debate regarding the use of pharmaceutical interventions for children with learning disabilities. Chapters 6, 7, and 9 infer that pharmaceutical remedies are an important intervention to emotionally disturbed children and youth.

New diagnoses and treatments seem to pop up on a regular basis, providing families and teachers with hope for a better answer. e*School News* (2003) describes the development of the human physical basis for a tool to diagnose ADHD. The physical differences between ADHD diagnosed and non-ADHD persons were observed through accidental findings by an Eastman Kodak Research team. Rather than rely on extensive observations over time by teachers and parents, this tool would assess the presence or absence of ADHD with a 10-20 minute test.

CHANGING PERCEPTIONS OF CHILDREN WITH SPECIAL NEEDS

These medical discoveries have enhanced the lives of many children. In addition, medical discoveries have kept alive more premature children and children inflicted with childhood ailments. These medical interventions may be adding to the increasing number of children identified with special needs (Premature Baby—Premature Child, 2002).

Another possible explanation for the rise of children with special needs may be better diagnoses. However, the significant increase in autism during the past 12 years does not seem to be attributed to either reason (M.I.N.D. Institute, 2002). The number of children diagnosed with autism is the second largest group of children with special needs, children with learning disabilities being the largest group.

As researchers and medical practitioners acquire more knowledge of a disability, the practice is to develop new categories and subcategories of disabilities. Currently, IDEA cites 13 categories. In 1960, learning disabled children were not categorized as having a disability and not counted among those with disabilities. This category now accounts for half of the children with special needs (National Center for Education Statistics, 2001). According to the Types of Learning Disabilities chart in chapter 5, there are now three major categories and eight subcategories of learning disabilities. In the category of major emotional illnesses, in 1960 bipolar disorder was described as one category of mental illness. Currently, Diagnostic and Statistical Manual of Mental Disorders (American Psychiatric Association, 1994) mentions several types of bipolar disorders. As a result of this differentiation, medical doctors are faced with increasing difficulties assigning a specific diagnosis or treatment. Medical diagnoses are made with tentativeness, and initial care is viewed as a trial treatment, not cure. Medical doctors often describe children as having multiple handicaps.

Therefore, educators and parents, noting so many different labels and multiple sub-categories, are beginning to recognize the uniqueness of each child. Based upon this recognition of differences rather than labels or categories, teachers and parents should consider an IEP for every child with or without a disability. As children with special needs are mainstreamed into the general classrooms, teachers and parents will focus less upon the "average" or "normal" type of child. The vision is that all children have special needs and instruction should be tailored to each child.

THE VISION OF FAMILY-SCHOOL CONNECTIONS IN THE 21ST CENTURY

The vision of family-school connections in the 21st Century portrays a collaborative working relationship between families and the school. This relationship rests upon mutual respect between members of both groups—the family members and the school's faculty.

This vision is reality at CHIME Charter School located in the San Fernando Valley north of Los Angeles, California. This charter school was founded in 2001 by a group of parents. The parents had children that attended a university preschool in which children with special needs were included within general education classrooms. All of these parents wanted their children to continue in this manner during elementary school.

The parents linked with a faculty member at the nearby state university, who ultimately served as the new school's champion. The parents and the university faculty designed the curriculum and basic policies. They then secured their charter from the local school district and state. The parents collaborated with a select group of teachers to design a school that fully included children with special needs into general education classrooms. The school has opened its doors to all children, including children with special needs from mild speech and language disorders to severe multiple disabilities. The required ratio is 20 percent children diagnosed with special needs and 80 percent general education students. The waiting list for this school exceeds the number of children in the school so the school is required by California law to select new children on the basis of a lottery for each group—the general education and special education. K-3 class size is limited to 20 children; grade 4 through 5 class size is limited to 25. Each class has a general education teacher, a special education teacher, and two paraprofessionals. In addition, the classroom activities are supported by trained parent volunteers, community volunteers, student teachers, and specialists from service agencies such as a speech pathologist, sign language interpreter, and Spanish language interpreter.

Julie Fabrocini, the school's vibrant director, asserts, "The home-school connection is crucial to each child in our school. Parents are the experts on their own child and are the lasting relationship in the child's life. We teachers are transient in these children's lives" (J. Fabrocini, personal communication, August 1, 2003).

An interview with this principal provides a rich tapestry of parent involvement activities. The best practices that are included in the first monograph in this series, namely *Promising Practices for Family Involvement in Schools* (Hiatt-Michael, 2001), were utilized. In preparation to work in this school, all teachers are provided training and exhibit a willingness to be collaborative with parents and the community. The school has institutionalized several family involvement processes and problem-solving techniques to maintain a high level of collaboration.

First, there are daily morning and after-school meetings. All staff regularly meet for 30 minutes every morning to focus on academic planning. At this time the general and special education teachers work together on the curriculum. Second, after school, everyone who has worked in the classroom during the day—teachers, parent volunteers, paraprofessionals, and service providers—meet to debrief. There is a formal protocol to assure parity of roles and positive feelings. Everyone speaks around the table and shares one success or challenge during the day. They must describe when the success belonged to the child and when the success belonged to the adult. These debriefing sessions each day are the basis for revision and curricular planning for the following morning's faculty meeting. Third, the school supports frequent IEP team meetings. The average number of IEP team meetings is one per month for each child. At these IEP team meetings, a discussion protocol is followed. First, the parent describes the successes of the child and program. Then the teacher and staff share their positive comments. Next the parents offer their present concerns. Finally, the teachers and staff voice their concerns. This sharing of information provides a rich foundation to discuss and collaborate on future revision of the IEP.

In addition, there are three regular and structured ways to communicate on a daily basis between home and school, assuring the realization of the IEP. Each student carries a student planning book home every night. That book contains teacher's comments to the parents and parent's comments to the teacher. During each day, the aide completes a standardized 4×6-inch activity-organized form on which she writes what the child did during the day. One copy of this form goes home with the student planning book and the other is placed in the child's IEP classroom log. Parents report that they use these forms to stay aware of child's day at school and to dialogue with the child about those experiences. For the teachers, these forms in the IEP log supply necessary information to assess the child's progress toward the goals written at the last IEP meeting. Also, children maintain a portfolio of their classroom projects and participate in student-led conferences with their parents. The special education teacher assists the children with special needs to make work choices and adapt the presentation format for the student-led conference.

The school door and the classroom doors are open to parent participation. Many parents serve as volunteers in the classroom. However, these parents and other classroom volunteers must participate in a two-hour inservice before working in any classroom. There are additional training sessions available to these parent volunteers on topics such as student learning styles, adaptive techniques, or behavior management. The teachers and principal encourage parents to share their talents, such as music or art, and work experiences within the classroom.

CHIME Charter has a parent resource room and a volunteer parent liaison. School newsletters and posters around the office depict regular and varied parent offerings. There are monthly parent education meetings featuring noted speakers. Each parent has prepared a video on their child, sharing valued information so that any member of the faculty or support staff may have access to that information. A parent volunteer staffs the library and coordinates its growing collection of these videos, books, and other resources.

Parents on the Board of Directors are on a par with university faculty and other community members. In addition, parents serve on the Administration, Curriculum, and Parent Partnership committees. The latter is the fund-raising group for the school.

The director sums up this model connection of school-to-home in this way, "CHIME Charter looks to the parents for understanding of our children and serving as school leaders. These parents have hopes and dreams for their children. We believe that the school is responsible in realizing these hopes and dreams" (J. Fabrocini, personal communication, August 1, 2003).

CONCLUDING REMARKS

IDEA is under re-authorization by the federal government at the time of publication of this monograph. There will be minor changes but there will be even stronger commitment to parent involvement, interagency support, and inclusion. The three volumes in the Family School Partnership series, namely *Promising Practices for Family Involvement in Schools* (Hiatt-Michael, 2001), *Promising Practices To Connect Schools With The Community* (Hiatt-Michael, 2003), and this monograph are available to serve as resources for parents and educators to meet these three critical components of IDEA.

REFERENCES

Adaptive Technology Resource Centre. (n.d.). *Technical Glossary.* [Online] Retrieved July 31, 2003, from http://www.utoronto.ca/atrc/reference/tech/techgloss.html

American Psychiatric Association. (1994). *Diagnostic and statistical manual of mental disorders* (4th Ed.). Washington, DC: Author.

American Psychiatric Association. Task Force on DSM-IV. (2000). *Diagnostic and statistical manual of mental disorders: DSM-IV-TR* (4th Ed.). Washington, DC: American Psychiatric Association.

Armstrong, T. (1994). *Multiple intelligences in the classroom.* Alexandria, VA: Association for Supervision and Curriculum Development.

Bush, G. W. (2001). *Remarks by the President in announcement of New Freedom Initiative.* [Online] Retrieved on July 26, 2003 from http://www.whitehouse.gov/releases

Byrnes, W. (Spring, 2003). A parent's view. *The Special Edge, 16*(3), 6-7.

The CHIME Institute. (2003). Quality education for all children. Available from CHIME Charter Elementary School. P.O. Box 280310, Northridge, CA 91328-0310.

California Department of Education. (n.d.). *Diagnostic center.* Retrieved October 31, 2003 from 222.dcc-cde.ca.gov/#about

eSchool News. (July, 2002). New tool could help curb ADHD: Kodak develops method for quicker diagnosis. *eSchool News, 6*(6), 1.

Hales, D. (2003, July 27). Who says I can't? *Parade Magazine,* 16-17.

Hiatt, D. B. (1971) Report of task force B: Education in 1980. In J. I. Goodlad (Ed.), *Schooling for the future: Toward quality and equality in precollegiate education. A report to the Presidents Commission on School Finance* (No. 9, pp. 28-29). Los Angeles, CA: Educational Inquiry, Inc.

Hiatt, D. B., & Keesling, J. W. (1980). *The dependability of classroom observations.* (ERIC Document Reproduction Service, No 175 929).

Hiatt-Michael, D. B. (Ed.). (2003). *Promising practices to connect schools with the community.* Greenwich, CT: Information Age Publishing.

Hiatt-Michael, D. B. (Ed.). (2001). *Promising practices for family involvement in schools.* Greenwich, CT: Information Age Publishing.

Johnson, D. W., Johnson, R. T., & Holubec, E. J. (1994). *The new circles of learning: Cooperation in the classroom and school.* Alexandria, VA: Association for Supervision and Curriculum Development.

Levine, M. (2002). *A mind at a time.* New York: Simon & Schuster.

Mayo Foundation for Medical Education and Research. (2003). *Attention-deficit/ hyperactivity disorder: Overview.* [Online] Retrieved from http://www.mayoclinic.com/invoke.cfm?id=DS00275

M.I.N.D. Institute. (2002). *M.I.N.D. Institute study confirms autism increase.* [Online] Retrieved August, 4, 2003, from http://news.ucdmc.ucdavis.edu/mindepi_study.html

National Center for Education Statistics. (2001). Federal programs for education and related activities (Chap. 4). *Digest of Education Statistics.* [Online] Retrieved on July 28, 2003 from http://nces.ed.gov/pubs2002/digest2001/ch4.asp

Office of Special Education Programs. (1999). *IDEA '97 introductory comments: topic brief.* [Online] Retrieved Aug. 4, 2003 from http://www.ed.gov/offices/OSERS/Policy /IDEA/brief1.html

Office of Special Education and Rehabilitative Services. (2003). Ideas that work. In *Idea '97 final regulations: Discipline for children with disabilities.* [Online] Retrieved July 28, 2003, from http://www.ed.gov/offices/OSERS/Policy/IDEA/

Office of Special Education and Rehabilitative Services. (2003). *IDEA '97: The law.* [Online] Retrieved July 28, 2003, from http://www.ed.gov/offices/OSERS/Policy/IDEA/the_law.html

Paige, R. (2003) Paige Releases Principles for Reauthorizing Individuals with Disabilities Education Act (IDEA). [Online] Retrieved on August 5, 2003 from http://www.ed.gov/PressReleases/02-2003/02252003.html.

Premature baby—Premature child. (2002). [Online] Retrieved August 4, 2003, from the Community website http://www.comeunity.com/premature/preemie-child/

Technical Assistance Alliance for Parent Centers. (n.d.). Homework support through technology is finally here! [Online] Retrieved August 4, 2003, from http://www.taskca.org

Tollestrup, B. (2003). Keeping disabilities from becoming handicaps. *The Special Edge, 16*(2), 16.

Tomlinson, C. A. (1999). *The differentiated classroom: Responding to the needs of all learners.* Alexandria, VA: Association for Supervision and Curriculum Development.

Zabala, J. (1996). Setting the stage for success: Building success through effective selection and use of assistive technology systems. In *Proceedings of the Southeast Augmentative Communication Conference.* Birmingham, AL

CHAPTER 2

HISTORICAL ANTECEDENTS, LEGAL ISSUES, AND GOVERNMENT POLICIES RELATED TO FAMILY INVOLVEMENT FOR CHILDREN WITH SPECIAL NEEDS

Leland L. Simmons

EARLY HISTORY OF EDUCATING CHILDREN WITH DISABILITIES

Historically, parental input and involvement was encouraged during the creation of the public schools in the United States. However, the movement to create a public school system did not include disabled children but rather was designed for "normal children." Public school in the U.S. has no strong tradition of inclusion (Taylor, 2000). Although the U.S. has

Promising Practices Connecting Schools to Families of Children with Special Needs, pages 15–24.
A Volume in: Family School Community Partnership Issues
Copyright © 2004 by Information Age Publishing, Inc.
All rights of reproduction in any form reserved.
ISBN: 1-930608-99-3 (hardcover), 1-930608-98-5 (paperback)

always had concern for the education of its young people, it should be remembered for the sake of this discussion that there is no federal constitutional right to education (Rothstein, 1995).

The approach to educating handicapped children has evolved slowly. During the 1800s, emphasis was placed on alleviating stress on mainstream schoolteachers and students by removing handicapped children from the mainstream classroom and placing them in separate special education classrooms or schools. After World War I and World War II, soldiers returned home with every kind of handicap: physical, mental, and emotional. Attitudes began to change about the handicapped, and U.S. citizens soon demanded that something be done to help the returning veterans. The parents of handicapped children observed the positive attitudes toward helping veterans with disabilities and demanded that something be done for their own children. There was still a long way to go toward public acknowledgement of the worth and dignity of those born handicapped (Rothstein, 1995). Strong parent involvement and support groups were needed to advocate for individuals with congenital disabilities and secure their rights.

As late as the 1970s, students with disabilities were routinely and legally excluded from school in the U.S. Once school officials had determined that a handicapped student was to be excluded, it was illegal in some states for parents to appeal or protest such a decision (Blenk & Landau-Fine, 2000; Rothstein, 1995; Yell et al., 1998).

Eventually, the main purpose and focus of education for handicapped children began to shift from separation toward teaching self-reliance. There was also a realization that segregation in the education process had some negative consequences. Special education began to undergo significant change in 1954 with the landmark legal case of *Brown v. the Topeka Board of Education* (Barbour & Barbour, 1997; Blenk & Landau-Fine, 2000; Fuller & Olsen, 1998; Rothstein, 1995; Simpson, 1996). African American children were being educated separately in facilities that were supposed to be equal to the school facilities of White children. However, this ruling recognized that the education of African American children was unequal, and that there was a stigma attached to being educated separately. The Brown decision set the precedent for the idea that educating handicapped children separately was harmful (Rothstein, 1995; Simpson, 1996; Yell, Rogers, & Lodge-Rogers, 1998). This ruling helped to promote the idea of educating children with disabilities in the mainstream classroom as much as is appropriate for each particular child.

EVOLUTION OF SPECIAL EDUCATION LAW

Parent involvement has been strong in advocating for disabled children. Parent groups, such as the Association for Retarded Citizens and the Association for Children and Adults with Learning Disabilities, were formed to campaign for the rights and pass legislation on behalf of disabled children. These and other organizations have been influential in advocating in the courts at the state and federal legislation levels. They have participated in congregational hearings and lobbying. A significant quantity of state and federal legislation has been passed as a result of the efforts of these parent groups (Rothstein, 1995).

Elementary and Secondary Education Act of 1965

The Elementary and Secondary Education Act (ESEA) was passed as a law that was to address the war on poverty. The educational programs that were funded with the passage of this act were Project Head Start, Chapter I/Title I Home Start, and Project Follow Through. These programs were designed to provide more equitable educational experiences to disadvantaged youngsters. Head Start was the most comprehensive of the programs because it addressed nutrition, health, and psychological services in addition to education. Active parent involvement was a strong component of Head Start (Barbour & Barbour, 1997). Project Head Start was also successful in providing services to handicapped children at the preschool level. Handicapped students attending Head Start typically already had services in place upon entering kindergarten.

The PARC and Mills Decisions

Two important decisions, *Pennsylvania Association for Retarded Children (PARC) v. Pennsylvania* (1971) and *Mills v. the Board of Education* (1972), set mandates for parents of handicapped children to have the right to due process pertaining to the labeling, placement of students in special education programs, and other potentially exclusionary phases of the educational decision making process. The Mills decision gave parents the right to appeal decisions about their handicapped child that they did not agree were in the best interest of the child. Parents received the right to have a hearing, the right have access to their child's records, and the right to written notice regarding all phases of the special education decision process (Blenk & Landau-Fine, 2000; Rothstein, 1995).

The Rehabilitation Act of 1973

Public Law 93-112, Section 504 of the Rehabilitation Act, requires schools and employers to make accommodations for disabled individuals. Eligibility under Section 504 includes "any person who

1. has a physical or mental impairment which substantially limits one or more of such person's major life activities,
2. has a record of such an impairment, or
3. is regarded as having such an impairment" (Rothstein, 1995, p.28).

The "major life activities" referred to can include seeing, hearing, speaking, breathing, learning, walking, and caring for ones basic needs (Blenk & Landau-Fine, 2000; Rothstein, 1995; Tayor, 2000). Students who are not candidates to receive special education services under other acts may still receive needed accommodations if identified as having such a limitation (de Bettencourt, 2002). Though Section 504 does not allocate funding, it makes it illegal for any education program that receives federal funding to discriminate against an individual with a disability. However, Section 504 does not give detailed guidelines for its implementation (de Bettencourt, 2002; Rothstein, 1995).

Education for All Handicapped Children Act of 1975

Public Law 94-142, the Education for All Handicapped Children Act (EAHCA), was the most comprehensive law for handicapped children that had ever been passed in the United States. This law guaranteed the following:

- That handicapped children would receive all the services and equipment that they need at public school in order to obtain an education.
- That federal funding would be provided toward this end (the first federal allocation of funds for this purpose).
- That the handicapped had the right to be educated in the least restrictive environment (LRE).

This meant that disabled students would no longer be confined to an environment with only special education students. If children with handicaps could viably be successful in certain subject areas outside of the special education classroom for specific parts of the day, they were allowed to be mainstreamed for that time (Fuller & Olsen, 1998; Rothstein, 1995).

One of the most significant aspects of EAHCA was that it gave continuity of services for children with handicaps from state to state. It also had strong provision for mandated parent involvement for the parents of handicapped children. Parents were now informed of every aspect of their child's education and their permission was needed before implementing any special education service to students with special needs. The mandates for parent involvement were taken from the Mills decision. In fact the Mills decision was incorporated into EAHCA (Rothstein, 1995; Simpson, 1996).

Individuals with Disabilities Education Act of 1990

EAHCA was amended and re-named the Individuals with Disabilities Education Act of 1990. It provides funding and regulates all special education services in the U.S. (de Bettencourt, 2002). The language changed from previous legislation in that children are referred to as having "disabilities" instead of "handicaps." The basic principles are stated below:

- All children with disabilities must be given education.
- It must be provided in the least restrictive appropriate placement.
- Education is to be individualized and appropriate to the child's unique needs.
- It is to be provided free.
- Procedural protections are required to ensure that the substantive requirements are met.

Individuals with Disabilities Education Act of 1997

Though IDEA of 1997 maintains many of the same features as IDEA of 1990, there are two important additions relevant to this discussion. First, the new act states that education for children with disabilities should be individualized as outlined in an Individual Education Plan (IEP). This plan is the product of collaboration among parents, the student, educators, and others who may offer valuable input, such as social workers, court liaisons, and mental health professionals. Second, the new act states that to the maximum extent appropriate, children with disabilities should be educated with children who are not disabled. It elaborates on this topic, stating that special classes, separate schooling, or other removal of children with disabilities from the regular education environment should occur only when the nature of severity of the disability is such that education in general education with the use of supplementary aids and services cannot be achieved satisfactorily. This applies to both public and private facilities (Department of Education, 2002, Rothstein, 1995, p.123).

The words *mainstreaming* and *inclusion* are not found anywhere in the IDEA statutes, but LRE implies that students with disabilities can be integrated into the mainstream program for their education, to the degree that the IEP planners believe will benefit the student. From this section of the law educators are able to infer and support the rationale for inclusive education (Tanner, Linscott, & Galis, 1996).

Reauthorization Status of the IDEA of 1997

The reauthorization of the IDEA of 1997 occurs every five years. The last reauthorization of the act expired in 2002. Currently, the IDEA of 1997 will continue until the new act is passed by Congress and signed by the President of the United States. The process of reauthorization is entering its final stages and will go to the floor of the United States House of Representatives for a full vote in January 2004 (idea.practices.org.2003 retrieved November 9, 2003).

The Inclusion Movement

In 1984, Madeline Will, U.S. Assistant Secretary of Education, called for the merger of special education and general education (Blenk & Landau-Fine, 2000; Ferguson, 1992). This cooperative merger between mainstream education and special education was the beginning of the controversy and discussion on inclusion practices in the U.S. (Rothstein, 1995; Simpson, 1996). Inclusive education has been the subject of legal cases and part of the discourse between parents, advocates, policy makers, administrators, and educators. The philosophy of placing students in a setting that is as normal as possible is based upon the following three principles (Rothstein, 1995):

- Separation in education is inherently stigmatizing to students with disabilities.
- Peer interaction is a highly valued goal for children who are disabled.
- Once a child is placed into a separate educational setting, the child will function and perform at a certain level and the expectation generally becomes a self-fulfilling prophecy when evaluating the child's performance.

Separation and Stigmatization

Rothstein's (1995) work makes an argument that segregating students also makes them feel different, perhaps inferior, by being excluded from the general education setting. Inclusion might alleviate this problem. Inclusion also allows children who do not have disabilities opportunities to have exposure to students with handicaps, which may increase their empathy and understanding. At the same time, the exposure may eventually decrease the prejudice or discomfort non-disabled students might otherwise feel when encountering disabled individuals in many settings.

Peer Interaction

Inclusion is also a means of helping students who may need additional stimulation but may not receive it sufficiently in a special education setting. Studies by Galis et al. (1995), Farber and Klein (1999), and Prelock, Miller, & Reed (1995) supported the efficacy of inclusion models of education. Some educators contend that a child's belief that he or she is entitled to a place in a community of peers is an important precondition for learning. Some educators believe that students with severe disabilities who have been placed into a general education classroom demonstrate better social development, more social interaction, greater skill acquisition and generalization, better health, more independence, and increased success in meeting the goals of the IEP.

Proponents of Full Inclusion

Proponents of inclusion envisioned that students with disabilities would be educated in the general education classroom all day. The call for the merging of special education and general education was based on the belief that mainstream teachers are equipped to meet all of the needs of all students with assistance and support from specialists (Rothstein, 1995). Inclusion proponents believe that these two separate systems of education are unable to respond effectively to the specific needs of both students with disabilities and students without disabilities who experience educational difficulties. Thus, they advocate a single system of education for all students that provides support for all specific needs from within the general education classroom. With flexible spatial-arrangements and instructional patterns, along with human and material supports for those with special needs, students with disabilities could be accommodated (Tanner et al., 1996).

Opponents of Full Inclusion

Opponents like Smietana (2001) argue that not all students should be in the mainstream setting. The environment should be appropriate for the individual student, and some disabilities require the specialized interactions and close monitoring that a special education environment can offer. The needs of non-disabled students should be considered as well. Factors such as a disabled student's insufficient cognitive development, socially inappropriate behavior, and/or disruptive behavior may preclude inclusion in general education classrooms. In addition, opponents question the assumption that separation in education is inherently stigmatizing. It may be that within a general education classroom, some disabled students may see a more stark contrast between themselves and their peers, so they may feel more comfortable and normal among similarly disabled students

Proponents of Partial Inclusion

The legal right to be educated in the least restrictive environment can be provided by partial inclusion programs. In addition, for many students, this arrangement can be the most beneficial. For example, Prelock et al. (1995) found that using the partial inclusion model for language-disabled students in particular was a viable way of imparting language services. This model appeared effective for several types of language disability areas: auditory processing, oral expressive deficits, semantics, problem solving, and critical thinking. The partial inclusion model of education provides students with continuity in both their mainstream curriculum and the specialized curriculum provided by speech language pathologists. In addition, students regularly have opportunities to practice and generalize newly acquired knowledge and skills in a mainstream classroom setting where they are exposed to normal communication patterns.

Opponents of Partial Inclusion

Galis and Tanner (1995) and Tanner et al. (1996) cited in their review of the literature and in their research that pull-out service delivery systems are not effective in remediation and habilitation of milder disabilities. They provide several reasons for this conclusion. First, there is often very little active academic instruction. Special education teachers are concerned with working on skills; instruction is skill based, and is not tied to the classroom curriculum. Students who participate in pull-out programs do not use or generalize these new skills upon return to the mainstream classroom. Second, special education teachers are less trained in the academic areas. Third, special education programs are generally lacking in a holistic approach to teaching. Fourth, students are served in small diverse groups from varying grade levels, so the instruction may often be below or too far above a specific student's level. Analysis of data indicates that students served in special education do not demonstrate the expected growth in achievement.

SUMMARY

In conclusion, parents have been part of the encouraging social and legal progress toward fully meeting the needs of disabled students. Although some schools have yet to fully implement their existing policies, most educators now take seriously the charge to ensure a quality and individually-tailored education for disabled students. Parents have been an important part of the continuing debate over the effectiveness of full and partial inclusion. At present, although additional research is needed in this area, it appears that partial inclusion should be considered among education's best practices, as an option that meets the specific needs of many students.

REFERENCES

Barbour, C., & Barbour, N. H. (1997). *Families, schools, and communities building: Partnerships for educating children.* Columbus, OH: Merrill Prentice Hall.

Blenk, K., & Landau-Fine, D. (2000). From segregation to integration: A brief history of special education and inclusion. In M. Philipsen (Ed.), *Assessing inclusion: Strategies for success* (pp. 11-37). Bloomington, IN: Phi Delta Kappa International.

de Bettencourt, L. U. (2002). Understanding the differences between IDEA and Section 504. *Teaching Exceptional Children 34*(3), 16-23.

Department of Education. (2002). *IDEA '97: Individuals with disabilities education act amendments of 1997.* [Online] Retrieved April 18, 2003 from http://www.ed.gov/offices/OSERS/Policy/IDEA/

Farber, J. G., & Klein, E. R. (1999). Classroom-based assessment of a collaborative intervention program with kindergarten and first-grade students. *Language, Speech, and Hearing in Schools, 30,* 83-91.

Ferguson, M. L. (1992). Clinical forum, consultative, services delivery: An introduction. *Language, Speech, and Hearing in Schools, 22,* 147.

Fuller, M. L., & Olsen, G. (1998). *Home-school relations, working successfully with parents and families.* Boston: Allyn and Bacon.

Galis, S. A., & Tanner, C. K. (1995). Inclusion in elementary schools: A survey and policy analysis. *Education Policy Analysis Archives 3,* 15. [Online] Retrieved April 18, 2003 from http://epaa.asu.edu/epaa/v4n19.html

Prelock, P. A., Miller, B. L., & Reed, N. L. (1995). Clinical exchange collaborative partnerships in a language in the classroom program. *Language, Speech, and Hearing in Schools, 26,* 286-292.

Rothstein, L. F. (1995). *Special education law* (2nd Ed.). New York: Longman Publishers.

Simpson, R. L. (1996). *Working with parents and families of exceptional children and youth: Techniques for successful conferencing and collaboration* (3rd Ed.). Austin, TX: Proed.

Smietana, M. (2001). *Inclusion and science education: Critical issues for science teachers.* [Online] Retrieved April, 18, 2003 from http://www.cedu.niu.edu/scied/courses/tedu532/inclusion_and_scien ce_education.htm

Tanner, C. K., Linscott, D. J., & Galis, S. A. (1996). Inclusive education in the United States: Beliefs and practices among middle school principals and teachers. *Education Policy Analysis, 4*(19). [Online] Retrieved April, 18, 2003 from http://olam.ed.asu.edu/epaa

Taylor, G. (2000). *Parent involvement, a practical guide for collaboration and teamwork for students with disabilities.* Springfield, IL: Charles C. Thomas.

Yell, M. L., Rogers, & Lodge-Rogers, E. (1998). The legal history of special education: What a strange trip it's been! *Remedial and Special Education, 19*(4), 219-228.

CHAPTER 3

A NATIONAL STUDY OF PARENT INVOLVEMENT IN EDUCATION OF YOUTH WITH DISABILITIES

Lynn A. Newman

Partnership between families and schools is important for all students, but it is particularly important for children with disabilities (Bauer & Shea, 2003; Spidel, 2000; Turnbull & Turnbull, 2001). Family involvement in their children's education is a core principle of the Individuals with Disabilities Education Act Amendments of 1997 (IDEA '97), formerly P.L. 94-142, the Education for All Handicapped Children Act of 1975 (EHA; Rothstein, 2000; Weintraub, Abeson, Ballard, & Lavor, 1976). As the first federal law mandating education for all children with disabilities, the EHA was a landmark bill that affected not only those with disabilities but their families and schools as well. One of the law's main tenets is parent participation in educational decision-making, including decisions related to evaluation, identification, placement, and services (Bauer & Shea, 2003).

Despite this long-standing commitment to family involvement, until now no national data have existed to describe the extent to which families

Promising Practices Connecting Schools to Families of Children with Special Needs, pages 25–39.
A Volume in: Family School Community Partnership Issues
Copyright © 2004 by Information Age Publishing, Inc.
All rights of reproduction in any form reserved.
ISBN: 1-930608-99-3 (hardcover), 1-930608-98-5 (paperback)

of students with disabilities participate in their children's education at school or at home. Differences in involvement have been observed in the general population among families of children of different ages, racial/ethnic backgrounds, household resources, and other characteristics. It has not been clear whether differences also occur among families of students with disabilities. Schools and others creating programs to promote family involvement have had little information to guide the development of programs and activities supporting family-school partnerships for students with disabilities.

This chapter provides a national picture of education involvement of families of students with disabilities, using data from two studies that are key components of a portfolio of longitudinal studies being implemented by the Office of Special Education Programs (OSEP) within the U.S. Department of Education. These studies are: the Special Education Elementary Longitudinal Study (SEELS) and the National Longitudinal Transition Study-2 (NLTS2).[1] Both studies include national samples of students with disabilities (SEELS n = 11, 512; NLTS2 n = 11, 272) and provide statistical estimates that generalize to the national population of students with disabilities and to each federal disability category individually. Initially participants were 6 to 12 years old for SEELS and 13 to 16 years old for NLTS2. Both studies are longitudinal; SEELS has three waves of data collection over 6 years, and NLTS2 has five waves of data collection over 10 years. These studies were designed to collect information about students from multiple perspectives, including those of parents, teachers, and students themselves. This chapter focuses on family involvement data from the first wave of telephone interviews with parents in both studies.

FAMILIES OF STUDENTS WITH DISABILITIES INVOLVEMENT AT HOME

Families support their children's educational development in several arenas: at home, at school, and in the community (Epstein, 1994, 2001). By maintaining a home environment that encourages learning and focuses on school-related issues, parents can convey their support for education (Epstein, Simon, & Salinas, 1997a; Simon & Epstein, 2001). Family involvement in learning and school-related activities at home can be demonstrated in a variety of ways, including talking with students about school and school events, reading to children, and helping them with homework.

Parents communicate to their children that school is important by paying attention to school issues and by asking questions and talking about their children's school day (Hoover-Dempsey & Sandler, 1995). Conversations about daily classroom events, projects, or homework assignments signal that education is valued and can be a strong predictor of student achievement (Balli, Demo, & Wedman, 1998). Reading to children at home has been linked to improved literacy skills and more positive educational outcomes (Adams, Treiman, & Pressley, 1998; National Center for Education Statistics, 1998b). Parents' investment of time in helping students with homework communicates the importance they place on schoolwork. Encouraging students to do their homework and interacting about homework can increase students' understanding of the content and skills entailed in homework assignments, as well as improve the quality of students' academic work and their attitudes toward school (Callahan, Rademacher, & Hildreth, 1998; Epstein, Simon, & Salinas, 1997b).

Elementary- and middle-school-age (SEELS study) as well as secondary school-age (NLTS2 study) students with disabilities live in households where conversations about their school experiences take place regularly; as presented in Figure 1, 90 percent of younger students and 82 percent of older students talk regularly about school with their parents. Families of children with disabilities in early elementary grades frequently read to their children; three-quarters of these students are read to by a family member at least three times a week. Families of students with disabilities also are involved actively in homework support. Almost all parents of those in the younger grades and three-quarters of those in middle and high school grades are involved at least once a week in monitoring and interacting about homework. More than half of the parents of younger students

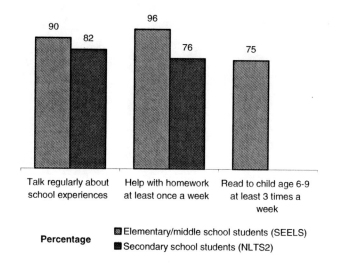

FIGURE 1
Support for Education at Home by Parents of Youth with Disabilities.
From NLTS2 and SEELS Wave 1 parent interviews.

and one in six parents of secondary-school aged students report assisting with homework as often as five or more times a week.

FAMILIES OF STUDENTS WITH DISABILITIES INVOLVEMENT AT SCHOOL

Families of students with disabilities also are very involved in school-based activities, although to a lesser extent than they are involved at home. Family participation at school provides opportunities for communication and interactions between staff and families, strengthening linkages between school and home (Hiatt-Michael, 2001). School involvement of families is linked to a range of positive outcomes, including improved academic achievement, better attendance, and more positive attitudes and behavior (Eccles & Harold, 1996; Epstein, 2001; Henderson & Berla, 1994).

Families of students with disabilities participate in a wide range of school-based activities, including school wide meetings (e.g. back-to-school nights and PTA meetings), conferences with individual teachers, and student or class activities (e.g. attending science fairs or musical performances; Figure 2). More than three-quarters of elementary and middle school-age, and more than 60 percent of secondary-school-age students with disabilities have parents who attend school meetings, conferences,

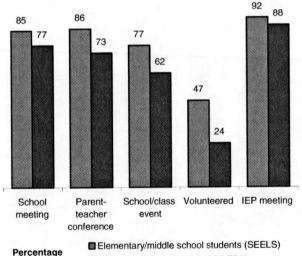

FIGURE 2
Participation in school activities by parents of youth with disabilities.
From NLTS2 and SEELS Wave 1 parent interviews.

and events. Parents also volunteer at school by being involved in activities such as chaperoning a class field trip or serving on a school committee, although to a lesser extent than other types of school-based involvement.

A type of family-school partnership specific to families of students with disabilities is parent participation in the development of their children's Individualized Education Program (IEP). The product of an IEP is a written document describing the student's level of educational performance; individualized, measurable annual goals; special education and related services; supplementary aids and services; and modifications and accommodations required to help the student meet their goals (Bauer & Shea, 2003). This document is created at an IEP meeting, which provides an opportunity for parents, the student (when appropriate), and school staff to communicate their preferences, needs, interests, concerns, and expectations (Turnbull & Turnbull, 2001).

IDEA '97 envisioned the IEP both as the means and the impetus for parents to become active decision-makers in their children's education. Parent participation is such a basic precept of IDEA that the legislation stipulates that if parents cannot attend the IEP meetings, schools must use other methods, such as individual calls or conference calls, and that schools need to take "whatever action is necessary to ensure that the parent understands the proceeding at the IEP meeting, including arranging for an interpreter for parents with deafness or whose native language is other than English" (Office of Special Education Programs, 2003).

When asked about their attendance at an IEP meeting, most parents of students with disabilities report having participated in at least one in the prior two school years. Although slightly fewer parents of older than of younger students report IEP meeting participation, this disparity in involvement between families of elementary-age and secondary-school-age students is much smaller than differences for other types of parent in-school participation.

Family attendance at IEP meetings does not always ensure active participation in the decision-making process. One-third of the parents of elementary and middle-school-age students and 45 percent of parents of secondary-school-age students report that their children's IEP goals were developed primarily by the school, with little family or youth input. For those who attended an IEP meeting, families of older students are much more likely to report being primarily responsible for developing IEP goals (21 percent) than their peers parenting younger students (1 percent primarily responsible). This difference may be due in part to students' assuming a more active role in the IEP process as they grow older; parents were asked to include youth involvement along with their own in describing whether the family or the school primarily had developed the IEP goals. Increased involvement of secondary school families in IEP decision-making also may reflect parents' increased skills, knowledge, and familiarity with the IEP process, after attending IEP meetings over multiple years.

When asked how they feel about their family's involvement in decisions about their children's IEP, about two-thirds of families, regardless of their children's age, feel they have been "involved about the right amount." Although the majority of families feel comfortable with their level of participation, one-third want to be more involved, and almost none would prefer to be less involved.

COMPARISON WITH FAMILIES IN THE GENERAL POPULATION

Families of students with disabilities are more involved than other families in supporting their children's education (Figure 3). They are more likely than other parents[2] to participate with in-school activities, such as meetings, conferences, and school events, and they are much more likely to help with homework. More than three-quarters of parents of secondary-school-age students with disabilities assist their children with homework at least once a week, compared with fewer than half of other families with similar-age children.

The difference in homework support is particularly striking for those who help with homework frequently. Youth with disabilities are markedly more likely to receive homework assistance frequently than are their peers in the general population. Only 16 percent of parents of elementary-school students in the general population report helping with homework five or more times a week (National Center for Education Statistics, 1998a), compared with more than half (55 percent) of parents of children with disabilities.

Often students with disabilities have more problems with homework than do their peers in the general population (Gajria & Salend, 1995; Polloway, Epstein, & Foley, 1992). Yet, even with differences in students' homework competencies, the fact that parents of those with disabilities are more involved than other parents is unexpected when considering the family demographics of the two groups. Families of students with disabilities are more likely than their peers in the general population to be living in poverty and are less likely to have a head of household who has attended or graduated from a postsecondary school (Wagner et al., 2003; Wagner, Marder, Blackorby, & Cardoso, 2002). Higher household incomes and parent education levels have long been associated with higher parent involvement (Lareau, 1987; Revicki, 1981). Yet, families of students with disabilities are more involved in their children's education than families in the general population who are more affluent and better-educated overall.

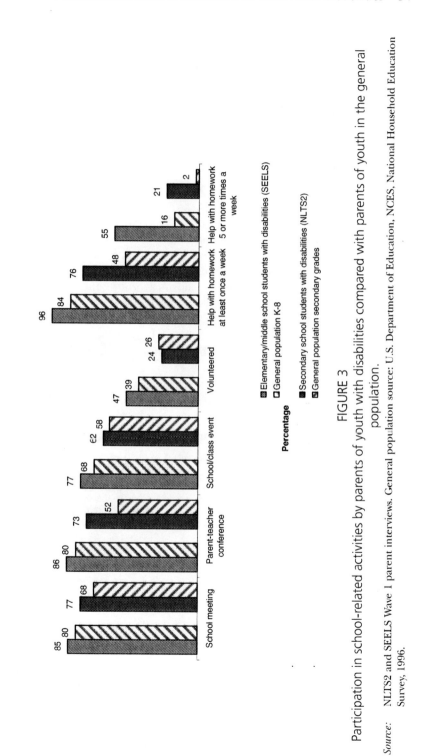

FIGURE 3

Participation in school-related activities by parents of youth with disabilities compared with parents of youth in the general population.

Source: NLTS2 and SEELS Wave 1 parent interviews. General population source: U.S. Department of Education, NCES, National Household Education Survey, 1996.

STUDENT CHARACTERISTICS ASSOCIATED
WITH FAMILY INVOLVEMENT

Students with disabilities are far from a homogeneous group. They differ in all of the ways other children do, as well as in ways related to their disability. Family involvement in education often varies by these student characteristics.

Grade Level

Family involvement both at home and school declines as children grow older (Table 1). Although family involvement decreases as students progress through the grade levels, the decline in family involvement is most noticeable during the transition from elementary to secondary school grades. Families of secondary-school-age students are less likely than families of elementary-age and middle-school-age students to participate in school meetings, conferences, and events, and almost half as likely to volunteer at school. The decline in homework support is particularly apparent for those who help with homework frequently. More than half of the families of younger students help with homework five or more times a week, compared with only one in five families of secondary-school-age stu-

TABLE 1
Youth Characteristics Associated With Family Involvement
in the Education of Students With Disabilities

	School-based Involvement	Homework Help
Grade level+		
Upper grades vs. lower grades	—	—
Disability related		
Lower functional cognitive skills	NR	+
Lower self-care skills	NR	—
Race/ethnicity		
African American vs. white	—	+
Hispanic vs. white	—	—
Gender		
Girls vs. boys (elementary/middle school age)	NR	NR
Girls vs. boys (secondary school age)	+	+

Notes: NR—not related; — = less likely to participate; + = more likely to participate
Source: Multivariate analysis of NLTS2 and SEELS Wave 1 parent interviews.

dents. This diminishing involvement of families of students with disabilities mirrors the experiences of their peers in the general population (Epstein, 2001; Stevenson & Baker, 1987).

Multiple factors may contribute to this decline as families and students mature and change, such as adolescents' growing need for independence; the increasingly technical content of homework, making some subject areas difficult for many parents; and the organization and policies of secondary schools (Brian, 1994). Schools attended by secondary-school-age students with disabilities employ significantly fewer strategies to reach out to families and encourage involvement than elementary schools do. For example, 44 percent of elementary-age and middle-school-age students attend schools that offer services to support parent involvement, such as childcare or transportation, compared with only 12 percent of secondary-school-age students.

Disability-Related Characteristics

The level of family involvement in home-based and school-based activities varies for students with different kinds of disabilities. There is much more variation between disability categories in some forms of school-based involvement than others. The most variation across disability categories is apparent in parent's attendence at school or class events, and volunteering at school. Students with speech or orthopedic impairments consistently have parents who are among the most involved. In contrast, parents of students with emotional disturbances are among the least actively involved in supporting education at home and at school.

Youth within each of the disability categories cannot be considered a homogeneous group. There are marked differences between youth within each disability category in their abilities and the difficulties they experience. One measure of ability involves the application of selected functional cognitive skills to daily activities such as reading and calculating. Another measure focuses on basic self-care abilities, such as dressing oneself or getting to places outside the home. When controlling for disability category and other student differences, those who rate lower on the functional cognitive skills scale are more likely to have parents who help them with homework. In contrast, those with stronger self-care skills are more likely to be helped with homework. Family involvement at school was not affected by these types of differences.

Race/Ethnicity

There are differences in some aspects of family involvement for youth with different racial/ethnic backgrounds. White youth are more likely than African American or Hispanic youth to have parents who talk regularly with them about school. In contrast, African American families, even when controlling for other family characteristics, such as income and education level, are more likely to help with educational activities at home than their white peers, although they are less likely to be involved at school. In this way, as in many others, parents of students with disabilities are similar to their peers in the general population, among whom parents of African American students also are more likely than parents of white students to help their children with homework (National Center for Education Statistics, 1999).

Gender

Although there are no significant differences between elementary-age and middle-school-age boys and girls in levels of family support they receive, by the time students with disabilities reach secondary school, parents of daughters are more likely to help with homework and to be involved at school.

FAMILY CHARACTERISTICS RELATED TO DIFFERENCES IN FAMILIES OF STUDENTS WITH DISABILITIES INVOLVEMENT

Beyond differences in their children's characteristics, families themselves differ in many ways, including their structure, parents' educational attainment, demands on their time, and supports they receive. Many of these family differences are related to differences in their level of involvement in the education of their children.

Parental Education and Income

Similar to their peers in the general population (National Center for Education Statistics, 1999), educational attainment and income of parents of students with disabilities are strong predictors of family involvement (Table 2). Holding other family and child factors constant, wealthier families are more likely to be involved at school, although they are less likely to be involved at home. Better-educated parents are consistently more involved in their children's education, both at home and at school.

TABLE 2
Family Characteristics Associated With Family Involvement in the
Education of Students With Disabilities

	School-based Involvement	Homework Help
Parent education		
Higher vs. lower	+	+
Income		
Higher vs. lower	+	—
Parent expectations		
Expect child to attend college	+	NR
Number of parents in household		
Two parents vs. single parent	+	+
Mother employed full-time outside the home	NR	NR
Other children in household with a disability	NR	NR
Belong to a support group for families of students with disabilities	+	+
Attend OSEP's Parent Training and Information Center trainings	+	+
Attend other trainings	+	NR

Notes: NR—not related; — = less likely to participate; + = more likely to participate
Source: Multivariate analysis of NLTS2 and SEELS Wave 1 parent interviews.

Parental Expectations

Research has demonstrated that having clear, consistent, and high expectations for students' learning and academic performance plays a key role in student achievement (Thorkildsen & Stein, 1998). Parents who expect their children to continue their education by attending a postsecondary school are more likely to be involved in school, although these expectations are not associated with involvement at home.

Demands on Parents

Parents need resources, such as time and energy, to be able to focus on school-based and home-based education activities. Students with disabilities living in two-parent households are more likely to have families who are involved in school-related activities than are their peers in single-parent households. Even when student and family background characteristics such as age, race/ethnicity, income, parents' education, and mother's employment are taken into account, families with two-parent households devote more time to their children's education. In this pattern they mirror the experiences of their peers in the general population, where marital status also is related to participation in school activities (National Center for Education Statistics, 1999).

The number of children in the household also can place demands on parents' resources. Secondary-school-age students with disabilities who have more siblings are less likely to receive homework support, although the number of siblings does not appear to be related to the level of home-based involvement for younger students. The relationship of number of children to school-based involvement is less clear, because parents could include visits to the school for other children in the family when describing school involvement.

Other demographic factors that one might expect to limit parents' time for supporting students' learning—such as mothers' being employed full time outside the home or having another child with a disability—were unrelated to the levels of support provided. Families were able to be actively involved in students' learning at home and at school, despite these potential limitations on time.

Supports

Parenting can be demanding, especially parenting a child with a disability (Bauer & Shea, 2003). Families may look for support in their parenting by participating in programs, trainings, and support groups for families of students with disabilities. Just less than one-third of the families participated in support groups and trainings. Some of these programs and trainings are provided by OSEP-funded Parent Training and Information Centers (PTICs) in every state. Almost 40 percent of the parents who attended trainings reported that they had participated in a training sponsored by a PTIC. Controlling for other student and family differences—such as age, disability characteristics, demographics, and family resources—families who either belonged to support groups or participated in training programs provided by PTICs, or other types of trainings, were more likely to be involved in both school-based and home-based activities. These types of activities can inform parents about how to create a home environment that supports school learning. They also can provide social support for doing so through reinforcement from other parents.

SUMMARY

Families of students with disabilities are very involved in their children's education, both at home and at school. Most families report regularly talking with their children about school, helping with homework at least once a week, and reading to younger children several times a week. Families participate in a wide range of school-based activities, including schoolwide meetings, parent-teacher conferences, and school and class events. To a lesser extent, they also volunteer at school. When compared with their peers in the general population, families of students with disabilities are as involved, and at times more involved, in school-based activities, and they are markedly more involved in home-based activities, particularly in monitoring, supporting, and assisting with homework. Families report high levels of involvement in their children's IEP development. Most feel they have been involved about the right amount in IEP decisions, although one-third want more involvement.

Both the kinds of disabilities students have and their severity are important influences on levels of family involvement. Variations in several other student and family characteristics, including grade level, race/ethnicity, gender, family resources, expectations, time demands, and supports, also are associated with differences in levels of family involvement. Most of the relationships of these family and student factors with levels of parent involvement mirror the relationships for their peers in the general population.

These findings raise concerns about both families who are highly involved and those who are less involved. Families were asked how satisfied they are with their children's school. The more time families spend assisting with and monitoring their children's homework, the less satisfied they are with their children's school. Homework help can be time-consuming and stressful, especially if parents feel they don't have the necessary knowledge and information to do it effectively (Bauer & Shea, 2003). For parents to support their children's homework activities successfully, it is important that teachers and parents remain in regular communication about issues such as the material covered in class, how homework should be completed, and teacher expectations.

Families who want more involvement in IEP decision-making should be provided with information, training, and guidance about the IEP process and the skills necessary to be contributing members. For those who are less involved in other school related-activities, research has found that school and teacher practices concerning parents are a more important predictor of family involvement than family characteristics (Epstein, 1990, 2001; Hoover-Dempsey & Sandler, 1995). Schools need to reach out to parents, especially targeting those who have been identified as being less likely to be involved in their children's education, because successful outcomes for children with disabilities require successful partnerships between schools and families.

NOTES

1. SEELS began in the 1999-2000 school year. NLTS2 began in the 2000-2001 school year. Both studies are being conducted by SRI International. SEELS and NLTS2 information and study reports are available at: www.seels.net and www.nlts2.org.
2. General population source: U.S. Department of Education, NCES, National Household Education Survey, 1996.

REFERENCES

Adams, M. J., Treiman, R., & Pressley, M. (1998). Reading, writing and literacy. In W. Damon & R. Lerner (Eds.), *Handbook of child psychology* (5th Ed., pp. 275-355). New York: John Wiley and Sons.

Balli, S., Demo, D. H., & Wedman, J. F. (1998). Family involvement with children's homework: An intervention in the middle grades. *Family Relations, 47*(2), 149-157.

Bauer, A., & Shea, T. (2003). *Parents and schools: Creating a successful partnership for students with special needs.* Upper Saddle River, NJ: Prentice Hall.

Brian, D. (1994). *Parental involvement in high schools.* Paper presented at the Annual Meeting of the American Educational Research Association, New Orleans, LA.

Callahan, K., Rademacher, J. A., & Hildreth, B. L. (1998). The effect of parent participation in strategies to improve the homework performance of students who are at risk. *Remedial and Special Education, 19,* 131-141.

Eccles, J. S., & Harold, R. D. (1996). Family involvement in children's and adolescents' schooling. In A. Booth & J. F. Dunn (Eds.), *Family-school links: How do they affect educational outcomes?* (pp. 3-34). Mahwah, NJ: Erlbaum.

Epstein, J. L. (1990). Single parents and the schools: Effects of marital status on parent and teacher interactions. In M. Hallinan, D. M. Klein & J. Glass (Eds.), *Change in societal institutions* (pp. 91-121). New York: Plenum.

Epstein, J. L. (1994). Theory to practice: School and family partnerships lead to school improvement and student success. In C. L. Fagngno & B. Z. Werber (Eds.), *School, family, and community interaction: A view from the firing lines* (pp. 39-52). Boulder, CO: Westview.

Epstein, J. L. (2001). *School, family, and community partnerships: Preparing educators and improving schools.* Boulder, CO: Westview Press.

Epstein, J. L., Simon, B. S., & Salinas, K. C. (1997). *Involving parents in homework in the middle grades.* Bloomington, IN: Phi Delta Kappa/Center for Evaluation, Development, and Research.

Gajria, M., & Salend, S. (1995). A comparison of homework practices of students with and without learning disabilities. *Journal of Learning Disabilities, 28,* 291-296.

Henderson, A. T., & Berla, N. (1994). *A new generation of evidence: The family is critical to student achievement.* Washington, DC: National Committee for Citizens in Education.

Hiatt-Michael, D. B. (2001). Home-school communication. In D. B. Hiatt-Michael (Ed.), *Promising practices for family involvement in schools* (pp. 39-57). Greenwich, CT: Information Age Publishing.

Hoover-Dempsey, K. V., & Sandler, H. H. (1995). Parental involvement in children's education: Why does it make a difference? *Teachers College Record, 95*, 310-331.

Lareau, A. (1987). Social class differences in family-school relationships: The importance of cultural capital. *Sociology of Education, 60*(2), 73-85.

National Center for Education Statistics. (1998a). *Digest of Education Statistics.* Washington, DC: US Department of Education.

National Center for Education Statistics. (1998b). *Indicator of the month: Early literacy experiences in the home. US Department of Education.* Retrieved June 27, 2003, from http://nces.ed.gov

National Center for Education Statistics. (1999). *Indicator of the month: Parent involvement in school-related activities.* Washington DC: US Department of Education.

Office of Special Education Programs. (2003). *Individuals with Disabilities Education Act (IDEA) 1997.* [Online] Retrieved June 27, 2003, at www.ideapractices.org/law/regulations/searchregs/200subpartC/Cse c300.345.php

Polloway, E. A., Epstein, M. H., & Foley, R. (1992). A comparison of the homework problems of students with learning disabilities and nonhandicapped students. *Learning Disabilities, 7*, 203-209.

Revicki, D. A. (1981). *The relationship among socioeconomic status, home environment, parent involvement, child self-concept, and child achievement.* (ERIC Document Reproduction Service NO ED 206-645).

Rothstein, L. (2000). *Special education law* (3rd Ed.). New York: Longman.

Simon, B. S., & Epstein, J. L. (2001). School, family, and community partnerships: Linking theory to practices. In D. B. Hiatt-Michael (Ed.), *Promising practices for family involvement in schools* (pp. 1-24). Greenwich, CT: Information Age Publishing.

Spidel, J. (2000). Working with parents of a child with disabilities. In E. H. Berger (Ed.), *Parents as partners in education* (pp. 367-413). Upper Saddle River, NJ: Prentice-Hall.

Stevenson, D. L., & Baker, D. P. (1987). The family-school relations and the child's school performance. *Child Development, 58*, 1348-1357.

Thorkildsen, R., & Stein, M. R. (1998). *Is parent involvement related to student achievement? Exploring the evidence* (Research Bulletin, 22). Bloomington, IN: Phi Delta Kappa Center for Evaluation, Development and Research.

Turnbull, A., & Turnbull, H. R. (2001). *Families, professionals and exceptionality: Collaborating for empowerment* (4th Ed.). Upper Saddle River, NJ: Prentice Hall.

Wagner, M., Marder, C., Blackorby, J., & Cardoso, D. (2002). *The children we serve: The demographic characteristics of elementary and middle school students with disabilities and their households.* Menlo Park: SRI International.

Weintraub, F., Abeson, A., Ballard, J., & Lavor, M. (1976). *Public policy and the education of exceptional children.* Reston, VA: Council for Exceptional Children.

CHAPTER 4

FAMILY INVOLVEMENT IN ADAPTING CURRICULUM ACROSS THE LIFESPAN FOR CHILDREN WITH SPECIAL NEEDS

Belinda Dunnick Karge

It is critical for families of all children, particularly children with special needs, to be involved in adapting curriculum in order to program their child for success across the lifespan. This chapter will suggest several strategies educators can use to motivate families to establish their own systems of family involvement from the time the child is born until the last stages of the education lifespan. Strategies include ideas for organizing the important information and documents, suggestions of ways to initiate home-to-school strategies, opportunities for participating in curriculum adaptation, and advice related to family support networks. Finally, family involvement at different stages will be explored, including early childhood, elementary, secondary, and adulthood.

Parents are the experts on their own children. They spend more time and many more years with their offspring than the professionals who are

Promising Practices Connecting Schools to Families of Children with Special Needs, pages 41–56.
A Volume in: Family School Community Partnership Issues
Copyright © 2004 by Information Age Publishing, Inc.
All rights of reproduction in any form reserved.
ISBN: 1-930608-99-3 (hardcover), 1-930608-98-5 (paperback)

paid to be part of the child's life. Parents and other family members provide key background information about educational needs and maintain threads of knowledge about the child. These threads are pieces of a tapestry, made up of information woven together by many years of successes, challenges, and resources implemented throughout the years. It is critical to document these threads to assist in curriculum history.

WHAT DOES IT MEAN TO ADAPT CURRICULUM ACROSS THE LIFESPAN?

Between 1900 and 1960, a Scandinavian philosophy termed *normalization,* was imported to the United States (Nirje, 1976). If, as our founding fathers wrote, an individual shared certain inalienable rights in common with all humanity, then by definition people with disabilities held the self-same rights as members of the same humanity. Educators, in regarding public education as an entitlement, are required to extend the prerogative to people with disabilities (Morgan-Rogers & Fuijoka, 2001). Persons with disabilities must live in the same society as their peers without disabilities. They use the same public areas, shop at the same stores, and are protected by the same fire and police forces as others in the area they live. They are people, and are not to be defined by a disability.

The Individuals with Disabilities Education Act (IDEA), originally the Education for all Handicapped Children Act (P.L. 94-142), ensures that all children with disabilities receive a free appropriate education in the Least Restrictive Environment (LRE). This law allows the opportunity for the child to receive the same supports and services as any child in the American school system. Deno (1970) introduced the Cascade System of Special Education Services as a model of service delivery to describe places where services are provided. This service delivery model has been adapted by schools nationwide and used as a guide to determine the appropriate LRE placement for a student with special needs. The service delivery begins with the general education classroom. This is the setting that is most similar to that of students without disabilities (Vaughn, Bos, & Schumm, 2003). Freeman, Alkin, and Kasari (1999) advocate for inclusive settings where children with disabilities have "real life experiences"(p. 143). This view parallels the normalization ideal. For many parents, greater levels of satisfaction were reported when their children received special education services inclusively in general education classrooms (Freeman & Alkin, 2000).

Students with special needs must receive adaptations, modifications, accommodations, and supplemental curriculum alongside their non-disabled peers. Wolfe and Hall (2003) introduce a *Cascade of Integration Options* designed to show how special education services can be arranged within the general education environment, with and without adaptations. When efficient progress is not being made, the Individualized Family Service Plan (IFSP), Individualized Education Program, (IEP) and/or Individualized Transition Plan (ITP) team might meet to discuss solutions. They may choose to move down (or combine) the full range continuum of the Cascade System from resource room services to self-contained classrooms, and in rare cases, continue on to non-public or home/hospital services. However, changes in placement alone do not guarantee educational success. Wolfe and Hall (2003) introduce a *Cascade of Integration Options* designed to show how special education services can be arranged within the general education environment, with and without adaptations.

Various curriculum adaptations, modifications, accommodations, and supplemental curriculum are often introduced very early in the child's life. *Adaptations* are instructional interventions that enable a child with special needs to more readily access curricular content or to more easily demonstrate understanding of that content. For example, using concept maps or graphic organizers, outlines, color coding, or highlighting text are all examples of adapting the curriculum. *Modifications* are interventions that include significant changes made to the curriculum, changes which enable a student to be successful in an education environment. For example, using a Picture Exchange Communication System (PECS) to structure the calendar for the day, or breaking the learning process down into smaller parts and teaching only the "big" ideas (Ellis, 1997). Fisher and Frey (2001) describe modification as "a change in what the student is expected to learn and/or demonstrate. A student may be working on modified course content, but the subject area remains the same as the rest of the class" (p. 157). *Accommodation* is an umbrella term for describing any of the supports a student receives in order to be successful in an education environment. The accommodation should be designed to provide the learner with adequate benefit from the instruction or situation with the least amount of alteration of the general programming (Smith, Polloway, Patton, & Dowdy, 2004). Handing a toddler your thumb to hold as she takes her first steps is an accommodation to the skill of walking. Fisher and Frey define accommodation as a "change made to the teaching or testing procedures in order to provide a student with access to information and to create an equal opportunity to demonstrate knowledge and skills" (p.157). For example, standard accommodations include using calculators or AlphaSmarts with a child with dysgraphia, or changing the font on an examination from 12 point to 20 point for a person with visual challenges. Sometimes the general education core curriculum and standards are not enough to support learning. In these instances, *supplemental curriculum* can be brought in to enhance existing instruction and curriculum. For example, the Read Naturally program (see www.readnaturally.com) is an excellent supplement to enrich growth in the area of reading fluency.

Supplemental curriculum is absolutely never meant to replace standards or the core curriculum!

Families must take a critical role in documentation and utilization of the variety of adaptations that were used across the child's growth years. In theory, the educational file located at the school (or clinic in some cases) should follow the child over time. In reality, sometimes files are lost, misplaced, or not forwarded when a family moves. Therefore it is the family's responsibility to keep more than just the traditional scrapbook of the child's photos; they must maintain student records and important documents.

ORGANIZING IMPORTANT INFORMATION

Early on, families should be encouraged to organize information about their child. It is suggested that families compile a notebook containing various sections, including but not limited to categories such as, medical, developmental, academic, emotional, social, and vocational history. Additionally, families should keep copies of Individual Family Service Plans (IFSP), Individual Education Plans (IEP), and/or Individual Transition Plans (ITP) concerning their child. This notebook should be used as a transition tool through the early childhood years, into the elementary, throughout the secondary years, and finally into adulthood.

Sometimes this organizational task can be very overwhelming. Simons (1987) suggests that parents think of themselves as the "case manager" for their child. Some parents may even see the task of organization of materials as their "job" on the IFSP, IEP, or ITP team. This takes the emotion away from the task and makes the time spent collecting and storing the information seem more worthwhile.

Medical Records

From birth, families should document all medical-related procedures. Any challenges during pregnancy, birth, or immediately thereafter should be recorded. Family members should be encouraged to keep track of every doctor and dentist visit, making notes on what procedures were performed. If the child takes a bad fall or has a severe ear infection, this may later be important information to the IEP/ITP team. It is important to document all immunizations, childhood illnesses, and treatments. The American College of Emergency physicians offers an emergency medical sheet for children with disabilities available free at www.acep.org. Anton (2002) suggests that families carry a list of all the child's critical information including medical history, prescriptions, allergies, and the pediatrician's name and phone number.

Developmental Progress

Documentation of developmental milestones (e.g. first smile, first step, age of first word) may become critical information as the child grows older. It is also important to document the family's living situation at the time of the specific developmental milestone.

Academic Progress

It is critical for all involved in a child's life to emphasize strengths. Unfortunately, many persons along the way will focus on the child's deficiencies. Family members need to emphasize and reward strengths and seek ways to expand and utilize exceptional skills. Parents might collect performance information, copies of student work, curriculum based assessments, standardized test scores, and copies of academic documents that show strengths. Documentation should include specific adaptations, modifications, and/or accommodations used to support the academic work. If supplemental programs are involved, it is important to document the names and references for the instructional programs for future reference. Parents might add information to be shared with educators, for example publications such as *What Do I Do Now? A Teacher's Guide to Including Students with Disabilities* (Giangreco, 1996) or *Instructional Management Tips for Teachers of Students With Autism Spectrum Disorder* (Marks et al., 2003).

Emotional Temperament

Every person has a personality that those close to them can acknowledge. Changes in personality over time can signal challenges. It is important for the family to document personality characteristics at each stage of the child's life and to take the time to write down specific emotions the child was feeling, or behaviors out of the norm.

Social Temperament

Are there certain factors related to the family's cultural, ethnic, primary language, or racial background that should be shared with educators and other professionals who work with the child? Social interactions can be influenced by how a child views the world through culturally-tinted lenses

(Barrera, 2000). Families should substantiate the child's likes, dislikes, and friendships over the lifespan. Keeping track of social activities, movies, and other extra curricular activities the child enjoys may support ideas for transition to the work force at a later date.

Vocational Planning

As of age 14, an Individualized Transition Plan (ITP) must be designed for all children with special needs. The focus of the ITP is to plan for transition from the education to the vocation. Job skills, career interests, and employment options are explored during this time and training implemented.

IFSP, IEP, and/or ITP Records

As members of the program planning team, parents are vital team players. It is critical that family members keep all written documentation summarizing their child's progress. It may be necessary to keep this information in a separate notebook along with a contact log of conversations and personal observations pre and post IFSP/IEP/ITP. If a parent liaison or advocate was in attendance at any of the meetings, ask them to document their perceptions and keep in notebook.

INITIATION OF HOME TO SCHOOL STRATEGIES

Research has concluded that parent participation in the education of children with disabilities is essential for the child to be successful and receive the proper LRE and special education services (Downing & Rebollo, 1999; French, 1996). Partnerships between parents, educators, and students can be formed if open communication and steady dialogue occur (Allan, 1997). Dunn and Fait (1989) describe partnerships using a data collection system called a "lunch box approach." The parents are trained in physical education skills to implement at home and assignments are sent from home to school via the child's lunchbox. This system of carrying a journal or note pad back and forth between the home and school can enhance home to school communication.

Parents and other family members should work on academic areas of weakness one at time. *In Helping Your Child With Reading Activities: A Parent Guide Book,* Sedano (2003) describes tips for reading at home and lists many wonderful books parents can check out from the local library. Many research based writing strategies can also be implemented at home (see Karge, 1998).

Parents must take the time to be involved in their child's education. *Involving Parents in Schools* provides many generic ways for parents to stay connected to their child's education by supporting the school environment (Steele, 1996). Research over the past several decades has documented that parent involvement benefits both the educators and the families involved (Henderson, 1987; Henderson & Berla, 1994). During 2001, parents from California met in focus groups to answer the question "What has to happen for your voice to be heard regarding your child's and other children's education?" As a result of this meeting, the parents' priorities for action were documented in a report *Partners in Decision Making: Parents Tell Us How* (see http://www.calstat.org/focusreport.pdf). The report provides many ideas for parent involvement in the education process.

Educators must take the time to get to know the parents and each child's individual needs. Lovitt and Cushing (1999) surveyed 43 parents of high school youth with disabilities; several parents commented that effective teachers took the time to know about the student's individual learning needs.

PARTICIPATING IN CURRICULUM ADAPTATION

Every child can learn. With enough time and curriculum adaptations, children can excel beyond expectation. For example, a child with mental retardation may need something to be repeated the same way, consistently, many times over a long period to eventually learn it. On the other hand, a child with a specific learning disability needs to see the same example in many different styles and situations in order to discover the format in which they can learn the information. This is the key to individualization of the curriculum. It is critical that family members use the strategies suggested previously in this chapter to ensure required documentation and a historical record of what worked and what did not work with the child.

Classroom Supports

There are some key research based classroom supports that can be used to enhance the education of children with special needs. These supports can be implemented by classroom teachers in large groups, small groups, and or individually. For example, Brophy (1981) suggests that praise is effective when it is for a specific accomplishment, offered to help the students understand the importance of their learning, and when it is recognized that this success will lead to other successes in the future (i.e. the ability to generalize). Another critical classroom support is involving families in all aspects of the decision making processes related to the student's education (Dinnebeil & Rule, 1994). Hanson & Lynch (1989) purport that each family is a system with all components interrelated, reminding educators they can not focus solely on the child without considering the family.

In 1994, Snell and Drake (1994) coined the term *supported education* to refer to general education classrooms with classroom supports including adaptations, modifications, and accommodations. Typically the classroom supports are designed so they benefit not only students with special needs, but also other students in the class (Stainback, Stainback, & Wehman, 1977). For example, providing a partially completed study guide for students to use during lecture or allowing students the option to tape their test answers or write them down helps all students focus and stay on task.

Classroom Environment

Students with special needs require structure and organized learning environments. When families visit the classroom, they should be able to see evidence of organization. For example, classroom organization could include: postings of clearly defined classroom rules, a daily agenda on the white-board, evidence of student work on the bulletin boards, and a display of clear classroom procedures. Parents can encourage teachers to add these components to their classrooms by volunteering to create a rules poster or make a bulletin board with every student's name on which to place student work. Parents can explain to teachers the critical need of most children with disabilities to have structure and organization in all parts of their lives.

Instructional Components

There are several key instructional components that should be used regardless of the disability or placement of the child. Special education is a service, not a place (Gartner & Lipsky, 2002). To really be special, the teacher must use research based effective teaching strategies. For example, Swanson (1999) synthesized the treatment outcomes for students with learning disabilities and found that "only a few instructional components increase the predictive power of treatment effectiveness beyond what can be predicated by variations in methodology and age" (p.137). These include sequencing, drill-repetition and practice-review, segmentation, directed questioning and responses, change in difficulty of a task, technology, group instruction, peer involvement, and strategy cues. Furthermore, Swanson (1999) purported that teachers combining Strategy Instruction and Direct Instruction witnessed the most gains in student outcomes. Teachers and families should become familiar with these techniques and use them consistently in their instruction of students with special needs.

Assistive Technology

The 1997 passage of IDEA mandates that assistive technology be considered for every child receiving special education services. These "considerations" must be documented (Lahm, Bausch, Hasselbring, & Blackhurst, 2001). This means that considerations should be discussed at each team meeting. The Council for Exceptional Children markets an *Assistive Technology Quick Wheel* to help parents and educators facilitate the considerations discussions (see http://www.cec.sped.org). Another resource for parents and educators is http://www.abledata.com, a site providing information on assistive technology and rehabilitation equipment.

FAMILY SUPPORT NETWORKS

There are many opportunities for families to participate in support networks. The most common types are disability associated support networks, or Internet support chat rooms and sites.

Disability Associated Support Networks

The Down Syndrome Society (http://www.ndsc.org) and CHADD (http://www.chadd.org) are examples of specific parent support groups identified throughout communities in the United States. There are many such groups for the wide array of disabilities nationwide. Support networks can provide you with reading materials, books, and some refer to experts in your local area. Carefully assess all material. Remember, if the author claims a magical cure, be cautious; most disabilities are lifelong and are not curable.

Internet Sites

There are many sites that offer information to the general public related to exceptionalities, for example, LD OnLine (http://www.Idon-line.org) and the Learning Disabilities Association of America (http://www.ldanatl.org/). Several sites can assist you in locating information about a specific disability. The National Institutes for Health (NIH) site (http://www.nih.gov) and the Parents & Educators Resource Center (http://www.perc-schwabfdn.org) can link you directly to support features and/or characteristics of a variety of disabilities.) For specific information on the Individuals with Disabilities Education Act visit www.ed.gov/offices/OSERS/OSEP.

Internet Support Chat Rooms

Simply inserting the disability name into a search engine on the World Wide Web will produce many sites. Choose your sites and sources of information carefully; it is often difficult to find research based answers. Families can ask specific questions by e-mailing www.eparent.com and the questions will be posted in *Exceptional Parent Journal.* LD OnLine (www.ldonline.org) offers the same opportunity for persons interested in Learning Disabilities.

A caution should be made that one of the most challenging situations for many families is making decisions on what types of therapies, social activities, and supplemental programs should be sought for their child. Typically, support networks are situation-specific and individuals share techniques and ideas that worked for their child with the other participants of the group. The danger in this is that just because the strategy worked for one child does not mean it is as effective with another. Professional educators should ensure that families are made aware of the limitations of support networks. Also, there are many programs available that have been highly successful with individuals, for example, swimming with the dolphins (Island Dolphin Care, 2003), yet no empirical research exists to validate the strategy.

FAMILY INVOLVEMENT PRACTICES
FOR DIFFERENT AGE GROUPS

In *Thinking Like a Lawyer: How to Advocate on Behalf of Your Child with Special Needs* (Ramos, 2003), Francisco Ramos Jr. states, "if we can educate ourselves about our children's conditions and special educational needs and approach our dealings with the school in an organized, professional manner, we can be more effective advocates for our children" (p.53). Ramos is a father of an adult with sensory integration dysfunction originally diagnosed at age 3. He recaps his family involvement throughout his son David's lifespan. The key points are very similar to those provided in this chapter. Ramos suggests parents learn to advocate effectively on behalf of the child by gathering information, organizing, reviewing, and writing "letters and memos to confirm the positions and promises of other parties" (p. 48).

The following vignettes share examples of situations in which parental involvement was critical in getting the support necessary to program the child for success. Parent involvement takes on different forms at the variety of stages in the lifespan.

Early Childhood

Juan was diagnosed with Pervasive Development Disorder (PDD) at 18 months. He attended a segregated self-contained preschool from age 3 to 5. He developed a very limited vocabulary and lacked language abilities. He was significantly behind his age appropriate peers. His parents moved to a school district that suggested he be placed in a general education kindergarten class with special education supports. The first month Juan's vocabulary doubled. He was so excited to tell his parents each evening what the children in his class could do. He had never been exposed to such a rich learning environment. The influence of the general education peers significantly supported his academic and social growth.

The most important decision parents make as a member of the IFSP team is where their child will receive special education services and what type of services the child will receive. Parents must weigh options, such as whether it better to get services alongside other children with disabilities in a segregated environment or to integrate with nondisabled peers. This is a very personal decision. Every individual responds differently to treatment and environments. Sometimes movements in placement can be very beneficial, as in Juan's case above.

Many research studies have documented parent participation in Early Childhood (See Dunst, 2002). Typically parents are active members of the multidisciplinary team learning to support a young child with disabilities. Unfortunately this changes as the child enters school (Dunst, 2002).

Elementary School Age

Emery is a third grader with Down Syndrome. He could not identify shapes, colors, or numbers nor could he read at the beginning of third grade.

Emery's parents requested he be placed in a general education third grade for "social" interactions. The resource teacher at the school introduced a new direct instruction approach to Emery. She collected copies of stories, finger plays, and puppets Emery liked from his past teachers and his family members. She used these familiar materials to teach Emery; first his colors, then shapes, numbers, and eventually sight words. Using examples and non-examples, the resource teacher sat with Emery in the general education classroom for 30 minutes every day. A sample lesson included many familiar items that were the color blue. She would pick up the item, point to the color and say "this is the color blue," pick up another item and state, "this is also the color blue.". . . Sometimes she would throw in a nonexample by picking up an item with another color and saying "this is NOT blue" . . . using this specific technique to teach one color at a time. Emery learned his colors one by one, one week at a time. Emery's parents also spent time with him, teaching the same skill the teacher worked on each week. At the end of 48 weeks, Emery now knows all colors, shapes, numbers, and 27 sight words. And he was invited to a birthday party and an overnight party for the first time. His third grade year produced more growth then he had during all past years.

Emery's parents worked with him every evening to support his successes. During the elementary years most parents are eager to do what is needed to help their child learn. Educators must ask parents to help and keep them in the communication loop with regard to what is taking place in their classrooms and the growth the child is making.

Research documents the intensive involvement the majority of parents experience with their elementary age child. However, adoption of family-centered practices similar to those used in early childhood intervention with multidisciplinary teams is virtually nonexistent (Dunst, 2002).

Middle School Age

Maria is a seventh grader with specific learning disabilities (SLD). She was not diagnosed until sixth grade. Prior to this, she had been very successful in school. When her first quarter marks were all failing grades, her parents called an outside consultant to come in and observe Maria both at home and at school. When the consultant arrived at the home, Maria was working intently on her homework, siblings were playing in a neighboring room, and her mother was cooking dinner in the kitchen. The consultant witnessed Maria's mother come into the living room where Maria was doing her homework and ask her to set the table for dinner. Maria appeared to ignore her mother. The mother asked four times, then out of frustration yelled at Maria to listen to her. . . . The following day the consultant observed a math class. Everyone was on task. About fifteen minutes into the task, the teacher asked the class to turn to page 318 and complete items one and two. Maria appeared to be on task until the teacher gave the instruction. As she looked over the shoulder of the student in front of her, the teacher indicated Maria needed to get back on task. It was determined that Maria had a processing disorder. She had not heard her mother or the teacher because she had trained herself to block out all distractions. When the pace changed in both situations, she was caught off guard. The consultant suggested a simple strategy. Anytime someone wants Maria's attention, they are to touch her on the elbow and wait until she looks up, then she will be ready to process whatever task she needs to do.

Family involvement studies of middle and secondary school is rare in the literature (Dunst, 2002). Unfortunately this means many parents are not in communication with the educators working with their children on an individual basis. And when communication does occur it is related to legal procedures (paperwork for assessments to be given, IEP or ITP meetings, etc.). Fortunately, the consultant Maria's parents attained was able to immediately support her and identify the current educational needs.

Secondary School Age

Jessica is a tenth grader with diabetes. She frequently has to use the restroom. During orientation, each of her seven teachers shared their procedure for what to do if you need to use the restroom when class is in session. However, three weeks after orientation, when Jessica was sitting in her third period class she had a hard time remembering which procedure was for the class she was in. One teacher had a ticket system, another wanted you to take the hall pass, another teacher had a sign-up by the door and one teacher had even said the students could not leave the room during the thirty minutes of class time. Unfortunately Jessica wet her pants while sitting in the class trying to recall the procedure. When a parent conference was called and the situation was discussed a simple solution arose. Each teacher agreed to the same system. The next time Jessica was in the situation, she knew what to do. Having a caring parent and a professional team working together provided a support network during Jessica's secondary years.

Secondary school is a time of independence. Many students do not want their parents attending classes or volunteering in the classroom. However, they want the support of their families and they need school-home collaborations.

Adulthood

James is a forty year old male with Cerebral Palsy (CP). He was educated in separated special education classes his entire K-12 educational years. After graduation, with the support of his family, James was able to learn independent skills and get accommodations to take college entrance exams. Currently, James is working on his second master's degree and teaching part-time for the local university. He lives independently. Sometimes he hires a caretaker to help him with everyday tasks and grading papers. He is able to drive with the use of an adapted vehicle.

Families should be encouraged to explore independent living options when their child is in high school or the early twenties. Independent living opportunities have expanded over the past decade. In Simons' book *After the Tears: Parents Talk about Raising a Child with a Disability,* an independent program director is quoted, "We have learned that a person with a disability, regardless of the severity, can live independently with support systems in the community. The important thing is for parents to realize this potential for their child, to prepare him for it, and not to limit the child's potential by assuming he can't" (Simmons, 1987, p. 64).

CONCLUSION

In 1989, the National Longitudinal Transition Study indicated that there was a direct connection to positive post-school outcomes when parents of children with disabilities expected their children to succeed and were involved in their schooling (as cited in Lovett & Cushing, 1999). Educators must work together to ensure that family participation is a guaranteed part of the team beginning in early childhood and advancing into the adult years. Family members will have valuable documentation regarding the historical perspective of the student's special education services and the variety of adaptations, modifications, accommodations, and supplemental curriculum previously utilized. Although family involvement may vary throughout the lifespan, it should always be encouraged.

REFERENCES

Allan, L. L. (1997). Food for thought. Do you resent and stonewall parents? *Young Children, 52*(4), 72-74.

Anton, G. (2002). Back toward normal: How our family recovered after Alison was born, *Exceptional Parent, 32*(12), 28-32.

Barrara, I. (2000). Honoring differences: Essential features of appropriate ECSE services for young children from diverse sociocultural environments. *Young Exceptional Children, 3*(4), 17-24.

Brophy, J. (1981). Teacher praise: A functional analysis. *Review of Educational Research, 51,* 5-32.

Deno, E. (1970). Special education as developmental capital. *Exceptional Children, 37,* 229-237.

Dinnebeil, L. A., & Rule, S. (1994). Variables that influence collaboration between parents and services coordinators. *Journal of Early Intervention, 18*(4), 349-361.

Downing, J. H., & Rebollo, J. (1999). Parents' perceptions of the factors essential for integrated physical education programs. *Remedial and Special Education, 20*(3), 152-159.

Dunn, J. H., & Fait, H. (1989). *Special physical education: Adapted, individualized, developmental* (6th Ed.). Dubuque, IA: W.C. Brown.

Dunst, C. J. (2002). Family-centered practices: Birth through high school. *The Journal of Special Education, 36*(3), 139-147.

Ellis, E. (1997). *BIG ideas.* Paper presented at the California Council for Learning Disabilities annual conference. San Diego, CA.

Fisher, D., & Frey, N. (2001). Access to the core curriculum: Critical ingredients for student success. *Remedial and Special Education, 22*(3), 148-157.

Freeman, S. F. N., & Alkin, M. C. (2000). Academic and social attainments of children with mental retardation in general education and special education settings. *Remedial and Special Education, 21*(1), 3-18.

French, N. (1996). Connecting teachers and families: Using the family as a lab. *Journal of Teacher Education, 47,* 335-346.

Gartner, A., & Lipsky, D. K. (2002). *Inclusion: A service, not a place: A whole school approach.* Port Chester, NY: DUDE Publishing.

Giangreco, M. F. (1996). What do I do now? A teacher's guide to including students with disabilities, *Educational Leadership, 53*(5), 4-16.

Hanson, M. J., Lynch, E. W., & Wayman, K. I. (1989). Assessing child and family needs. In M. J. Hanson & E. W. Lynch (Eds.), *Early intervention: Implementing child and family services for infants and toddlers who are at-risk or disabled* (pp. 130-154). Austin, TX: Pro-Ed.

Henderson, A. (1987). *The evidence continues to grow: Parent involvement improves student achievement.* Columbia, MD: National Committee for Citizens in Education.

Henderson, A., & Berla, N. (Eds.). (1994). *A new generation of evidence: The family is critical to student achievement.* Washington, DC: National Committee for Citizens in Education, Center for Law and Education.

Island Dolphin Care. (2003). Dolphin Magic. *Exceptional Parent, 33*(3), 80-82.

Karge, B. D. (1998). Knowing what to teach: Using Authentic assessment to improve classroom instruction. *Reading & Writing Quarterly, 14*(3), 319-331.

Lahm, E. A., Bausch, M. E., Hasselbring, T. S., & Blackhurst, A. E. (2001). National assistive technology research institute. *Journal of Special Education Technology, 16*(3), 19-26.

Lovitt, T. C., & Cushing, S. (1999). Parents of youth with disabilities: Their perceptions of school programs. *Remedial and Special Education, 20*(3), 134-142.

Marks, W. U., Shaw-Hegwer, J., Schrader, C., Longaker, T., Peters, I., Powers, F., et al. (2003). Instructional management tips for teachers of students with autism spectrum disorder. *Teaching Exceptional Children, 35*(4), 50-54.

Morgan-Rogers, A., & Fujioka, C. (2001). *Collaborative co-teaching: Creative solutions for teaming between general and special educators.* Unpublished Master's Thesis, California State University, Fullerton.

Nirje, B. (1976). The normalization principle. In R. B. Kugel & A. Shearer (Eds.), *Changing Patterns in Residential Services for the Mentally Retarded* (Rev. Ed., pp. 35-46). Washington DC: President's Committee on Mental Retardation.

Ramos, F. (2003). Thinking like a lawyer: How to advocate on behalf of your child with special needs. *Exceptional Parent, 33*(2), 48-53.

Sedano, M. (2003). *Helping your child with reading activities: A parent guide book.* Unpublished Master's Thesis. California State University, Fullerton.

Simons, R. (1987). *After the tears: Parents talk about raising a child with a disability.* San Diego: Harcourt Brace & Company.

Smith, T., Polloway, E., Patton, J. U., & Dowdy, C. (2004). *Teaching students with special needs in inclusive settings.* Boston: Pearson.

Snell, M., & Drake, G. P. (1994). Replacing cascades with supported education. *Journal of Special Education, 27,* 393-409.

Stainbeck, W. C., Stainbeck, S., & Wehman, P. (1997). Toward full inclusion into general education. In P. Wehman (Ed.), *Exceptional individuals in school, community, and work* (pp.531-557). Austin, TX: Pro-Ed.

Steele, K. (1996). *Involving Parents in Schools.* Marlon, IL: Pieces of Learning.

Swanson, H. L. (1999). Instructional components that predict treatment outcomes for students with learning disabilities: Support for a combined strategy and direct instruction model. *Learning Disabilities Research and Practice, 14*(3), 129-140.

Vaughn, S., Bos, C. S., & Schumm (2003). *Teaching exceptional, diverse, and at-risk students in the general education classroom.* Boston: Allyn and Bacon.

Wolfe, P. S., & Hall, T. E. (2003). Making inclusion a reality for students with severe disabilities. *Teaching Exceptional Children, 35*(4), 56-61.

CHAPTER 5

HELPING CHILDREN WITH LEARNING DISABILITIES SUCCEED
The Family-School Connection

Rosalyn Anstine-Templeton and Michelle A. Johnston

When Christopher Boyle was assigned to my class in second grade, I could see immediately that he was a bright, articulate boy. But it also became clear that he had the classic signs of dyslexia. He couldn't even write his own name without leaving out letters or reversing them. What I didn't understand was why he was such a behavior problem—belligerent, moody, easily upset.

I decided to call his mother to see if she could help me. She was more than willing to meet with me and offered to come in that very afternoon. Almost as soon as we sat down, Mrs. Boyle described how every night Christopher would sit at his desk and try to do his homework and cry and say how dumb he was.

Suddenly, I understood what was going on. He was mad because he was convinced he was dumb and was taking it out on himself and everyone else. [Together, we developed an integrated school-home plan to link his special

Promising Practices Connecting Schools to Families of Children with Special Needs, pages 57–77.
A Volume in: Family School Community Partnership Issues
Copyright © 2004 by Information Age Publishing, Inc.
All rights of reproduction in any form reserved.
ISBN: 1-930608-99-3 (hardcover), 1-930608-98-5 (paperback)

interests to learning and build his self-confidence.] At our next conference, Mrs. Boyle told me that he was like a different child at home. Much happier, much more relaxed, and eager to share his knowledge; [it was the same at school.] (Faber, Mazlish, Nyberg, & Anstine-Templeton, 1996, pp. 256-257).

Children with academic, social, and emotional disabilities (see Types of Learning Disabilities Chart at end of chapter) can succeed academically at school when families and schools form partnerships. With the reauthorization of Individuals with Disabilities Education Act (IDEA) in 1997, early childhood special educators initiated a family-centered approach to educating young children with special learning needs. This model is slowly reaching into other grade levels within education. In a family-centered approach, families become active partners in the learning process by being involved in the assessment, goal setting, and program implementation processes (O'Shea, O'Shea, Algozzine, & Hammitte, 2001).

In addition to being mandated by changes in special education law (Individuals with Disabilities Education Act, 1997), partnerships between families and school have proven extremely effective in increasing academic achievement, building parental understanding of and support for school functions, improving educators' job satisfaction, and raising the success rate of school programs (Robinson & Fine, 1994).

PARTNERSHIP SKILLS FOR EFFECTIVELY EDUCATING LEARNERS WITH SPECIAL NEEDS

Five specific skills are required to develop partnerships that enable learners with disabilities to succeed at home, in school, and in the community (adapted from Dettmer, Thurston, & Dyck, 2002, pp. 130-148). First, rapport-building skills are needed to build trust, and develop mutual respect for one another and each other's differences. Characteristics such as empathy, positive attitude, and a desire to help, greatly enhance one's ability to develop rapport.

Second, listening skills are required for communication. These skills include listening actively, observing body language and voice tone/inflection, and repeating to the speaker your understanding of the message.

Third, assertiveness skills consisting of a firm, confident voice, eye contact, and body posture that is receptive to the message receiver are important. It helps to use "I" messages and stay away from words with a negative connotation like *but*, *can't*, and *shouldn't*. The best practice is to be honest and acknowledge personal feelings or opinions.

Fourth, conflict management skills are needed if individuals become resistant, defensive, or angry. A skilled conflict manager knows how to handle his or her own defensiveness and knows when to stop pushing an issue by staying calm, controlling reactions, and listening.

Fifth, collaborative problem-solving skills, including supporting and showing respect, are needed to resolve problems. The most effective problem solving methods include establishing a pattern of listening, asserting one's ideas, and then listening again until all individuals have spoken and have been heard. It is best to remain focused on the goal (developing optimal learning outcomes for children and youth with special needs), rather than focusing on ones own emotions or opinions.

For successful partnerships to form, the "Stop, look, and listen" rule should apply: stop talking, look at the end goal, and listen to individuals who work with children and youth with special needs. The skills noted above are important for families and schools in forming collaborative relationships. However, the following suggestions are more specific to families of children with disabilities, followed by partnership ideas specific to educators.

PARTNERSHIP SUGGESTIONS FOR PARENTS

Faber et al. (1996) cite one parent's frustration.

> How come I feel as if I have to walk on eggs before daring to make the smallest suggestion? Because if, heaven forbid, I happen to offend the teacher by hinting she do something differently, and she gets angry at me, I know darn well she'll take it out on my kid (p. 231).

Families must take an active role in the special education process of their youngsters (Knoblauch & McLane, 1999). The role should be one in which families and "communities are understood to be equal contributors of understanding, knowledge, and skills to the educative process" (Hulsebosch & Logan, 1998, p.32). Without this involvement, children will lack an important advocate in the development of an individual educational program (IEP) that meets their specific learning needs.

Special education experts (Hulsebosch & Logan, 1998; Knoblauch & McLane, 1999; Rich, 1998) make several recommendations for parents to ensure effective participation in the educational process:

Parent Guidelines

- Become familiar with the child's Due Process Rights and Responsibilities that the schools must make available.

- Find a support group to share knowledge and experiences.
- Share information about the child's development and education (any medical records, past school records, test/evaluation results) during the initial stages of planning for an IEP.
- List things for the child to learn and explain what strategies have and have not worked at home. Ensure that IEP objectives are specific and measurable by reviewing the IEP at home and asking for clarification before signing. (Families have 10 days in which to make a decision.)
- Ensure that the school includes the child in as many regular school activities as possible such as recess, lunch, music, physical education, and art.
- Find out what services (group therapy, speech therapy, or reading) will be provided and ask how the services will help the child improve.
- Monitor the child's progress and ask for periodic updates. If a part of the IEP is not working, discuss a possible modification. Try to solve problem issues directly with the school.
- Keep notes and records of meetings and conversations.

Educators have been mandated to encourage the involvement of families and communities in the schooling of those with special needs. With IDEA 1997, families have many more choices, opportunities, and responsibilities in planning the special education process for their youngsters.

PARTNERSHIP SUGGESTIONS FOR EDUCATORS

I've had parents who were a joy to work with, but there are some with whom I would hesitate to bring up a problem. I told one father that his son was disruptive and that night the son got a beating. And right now I have a couple who are in the middle of a custody fight. It's obvious to me that their child has some serious issues, but during the conference all they did was blame each other and tried to get me to take sides (adapted from Faber et al., 1996. pp. 256-257).

To avoid the above scenario, administrators, teachers, and school personnel should see themselves as community builders in which people listen to each other and care for one another (Peterson & Hittie, 2003). Families who have children with special needs often become hypersensitive to environmental reactions related to their children. The looks of disgust or pity, negative head-shaking or eye rolling, or demeaning comments about learning or behavior cause many families to mistrust their children's educators (Peterson & Hittie, 2003). Therefore, educators have to build rapport with families. In building a trusting partnership with families of children with special needs, Davern (1996) recommends that educators

a. convey consistent messages regarding the value of the child,
b. put yourself in the shoes of the family members—they want to know educators are trying to understand what it is like to have a child with a disability,
c. show an authentic interest in the family's goal for the child,
d. develop a deeper understanding of cultural diversity and family diversity,
e. challenge stereotypes, and
f. talk with families about how they want to share information—use everyday language that does not make family members feel excluded.

Once families feel comfortable, educators can use the following strategies to help families with their child's IEP (adapted from Rich, 1998, pp. 77-80):

- Suggest ways for families to expand their children's learning experiences.
- Give families information about learning contained in articles and books.
- Help families access community services and other parents of children with disabilities.
- Encourage family members to be involved with their child's school.
- Invite businesses, senior citizens, and service organizations to provide mentoring or resources.

With productive partnerships, families and educators can more efficiently use their time and energies to create optimal learning environments for those with special needs.

CREATING OPTIMAL SPECIAL NEEDS LEARNING ENVIRONMENTS

When creating successful learning environments for people with learning difficulties, close attention should be given to the design of space, development of structures and routines, and use of instructional accommodations. In this context the learning environment includes home, school, and community.

Before examining the physical (visible) aspects of an effective learning space, the non-visible environment, or climate, must be discussed. What creates a positive learning ambience? The climate of a productive learning environment is not often given much thought. Yet, it is the vital component needed in any learning situation for individuals with learning difficulties. A successful learning environment for students with special needs has specific positive characteristics. It should make students feel welcomed and it should minimize the child's feelings of being different from peers. The environment must be comfortable and the learning space should provide students with a sense of independence, comfort, support, and security. It should be stimulating and motivating but not overwhelming or distracting (adapted from Clayton & Forton, 2001, p.120). Perhaps most importantly, the environment should be a place where respect is the norm, adults are enthusiastic and caring, praise is frequent, and social-emotional skills are taught (Anstine-Templeton, 2003; Sousa, 2001).

The physical aspects of the learning environment for those with academic, social, and emotional learning difficulties should accommodate learners' special needs. For the classroom, the space and arrangement should be flexible, so it can be arranged quickly to meet learning needs of large or small groups, partners, or individuals. Often, classrooms can be rearranged for active learning, where learning can be accomplished in a variety of ways for the most productive special needs environment (Clayton & Forton, 2001; Hartmann, 1993). However, a word of caution is worth mentioning. If this active-learning room arrangement is to work well, educators should make adaptations to meet specific learning needs. In other words, allowing a student to work in a group or with a partner is not a cure-all to his or her academic difficulties. It may help to incorporate modifications into the classroom, such as seating easily distracted students in areas that are free from distractions. When independent work time is required, study carrels may be needed.

Another classroom and home modification is the creation of a soothing "quiet zone" that children may use to be alone. This is especially good for those students who are impulsive or explosive and need time to calm down, gain composure, get self control, reflect on behavior or refocus on learning.

An area where private conversations can take place should be incorporated into the learning environment. For children with academic, social, and emotional learning difficulties, teachers will spend a good amount of time teaching how to express feelings appropriately, share strong emotions with others, problem solve, and be assertive.

Disorganization and clutter can frustrate and distract learners with special needs. Both parents and educators should consider organizing and clearing the learning environments by creating storage spaces for materials. Experts suggest keeping learners' work as free of unnecessary materials as possible (Anstine-Templeton, 1995; Clayton & Forton, 2001; Sousa, 2001).

It is recommended that the home learning environments also be adapted to the child's specific learning needs. Each child should have his or her own learning space that is free of distractions, comfortable, well organized, and supplied with needed materials (Warger, 2001). Home learning environments are unique to each family, so it is difficult to define what the optimal learning environment should look like. Some families gather around the table to complete homework or paper work, while others have individual desks in their bedrooms or home offices. Although the configuration of learning spaces at home may vary, there is one constant requirement—families are involved in the learning process. Research indicates the more the family is engaged in the child's education, the more successful the child will be at school (Haury & Milbourne, 1999).

Families and educators must share their observations of the child's specific learning space preferences. Teachers observe youngsters in school for six hours daily and can be extremely helpful in suggesting ways families can create optimal learning environments at home. Families know their children intimately and can help the teacher fine-tune the classroom environment to meet their children's specific academic, social, or emotional needs. Once the learning environment has been designed for productive learning, families and educators can implement structures and routines that will keep learners with academic, social, and emotional special needs on task and motivated (Hartmann, 1993).

STRUCTURES AND ROUTINES

Most individuals with academic, social, or emotional difficulties fail academically because the symptoms of their disabilities interfere with the learning process (Sousa, 2001). Learning is hindered by distractibility, short attention span, disorganization, difficulty following directions, frustration, and impulsivity (Peterson & Hittie, 2003; Sousa, 2001; Wicks-Nelson & Israel, 2003). Experts suggest that, to compensate for these behaviors, teachers incorporate ways to organize and structure the learning environment. (Anstine-Templeton, 2003; Hartmann, 1993; Jones & Jones, in press; Sousa, 2001).

Ways to Structure the Learning Environment

- Allow time for straightening and cleaning disorderly learning areas. A clean-up period gives children time to detach mentally from one activity and to focus on another.
- Display and review rules, procedures, and schedules to help children remember and follow them.
- Help the child create organizing forms, for example making checklists, developing timelines for projects, constructing daily schedules,

helping learners assemble assignment-tracking notebooks in order to promote organizational skills.
- Spend time monitoring activities, answering questions, and adjusting the program as necessary.
- Minimize distractions such as traffic noise, ventilators, television, loud music, talking, and appliances.

To reduce frustration that may lead to noncompliance, add structures that give learners time to make transitions from one activity to another. Be sure to count down the end of each activity—giving learners ten and five minute warnings. For school, use signals to get learners' attention—hand signals, lights turned off, or clapping a rhythm. For home, use a gentle touch on the shoulder or pat on the arm to get a child's attention or to refocus him or her on learning. Incorporating structures will ensure that children and youth will be able to focus on learning rather than using mental energies to figure out what to do next.

INSTRUCTIONAL ACCOMMODATIONS

Another way to make learning easier for those with learning difficulties is to make instructional accommodations. Although many of the instructional suggestions (Sousa, 2001; Vaughn, Bos, & Schumm, 2003) that follow are intended for teachers in the classroom environment, they can easily be adapted for use by the parents in the home.

- Be clear, consistent, and positive with directions. Explain expectations. Stand near individuals who lose focus when directions are given. Have directions prepared in a visual format.
- Use hands-on activities whenever possible. The skill is to keep learning interesting (so learners do not act out due to boredom), yet structured to avoid chaos. Schedule academic subjects in the morning if possible and allow for frequent breaks throughout the day.
- Incorporate technology into learning whenever possible. Use computers for drill and practice, which will often motivate people who become bored easily with paper-pencil tasks. Reluctant writers will use word processing programs because spelling, grammar, and punctuation are easy to correct. Individuals capable of high-level mathematics but who struggle with computation can use calculators to practice their strengths.
- Teach and practice the steps of cooperative learning and use it often. Children and youth with academic, social, and emotional difficulties lack skills to work collaboratively, so use cooperative learning to teach social and academic skills. With cooperative learning, students can be

put in heterogeneous groups to benefit from each other's learning strengths.

- Teach learners ways to take responsibility for their own learning and to use self-monitoring strategies. Allow individuals to complete their own checklists, timelines, assignment notebooks, time on tasks sheets, et cetera. Give opportunities for learning in new ways and with a broad range of topics.

- Use peer tutoring to help compensate for learners' areas of weakness. Peer tutoring systems are productive if the helpers have been trained and are closely monitored by the adult. Also, the one tutored has to have his or her progress supervised to make sure advancement occurs.

In the final section, issues will be discussed that sometimes cause productive partnerships and optimal learning environments to deteriorate. One constant in the lives of those with learning difficulties is that issues among adults will surface. How these differences of opinion, values, and philosophies are resolved will determine if the youngster's needs are met.

RESOLVING TENSIONS THAT SURFACE IN FAMILY-SCHOOL RELATIONSHIPS

Families and schools planning educationally for children and youth with academic, social, and emotional learning difficulties will (at times) find themselves at odds with each other. These tensions often surface around such issues as homework, behavior, or medication and must be resolved or negotiated so learners will succeed. Following are strategies for families and educators to use to avoid conflicts in these sensitive areas.

Homework Strategies

What really galls me is that [some] teachers feel no sense of responsibility to communicate with parents. I never hear from them until the problem is so serious that it would take a miracle to fix it, like when Michael was in junior high and he stopped doing his social studies homework. The teacher couldn't be bothered to inform me of that fact until the week before report cards came out. How's a kid suppose to make-up fifteen assignments in one week? (Faber et al. 1996, p.232)

Family members and teachers should discuss expectations surrounding homework. On the one hand, many families have strong opinions on the amount of time children and youth should spend doing school related learning at home. Researchers (Rivera & Smith, 1997) suggest that elementary aged children spend up to one hour on assignments at home and that adolescents devote up to two hours on homework nightly. On the other hand, educators have various expectations for completing homework and often anticipate an extension or practice of learning at home (Petersen & Hittie, 2003; Rivera & Smith, 1997). When expectations between families and schools differ, problems often surface.

Homework becomes a serious problem for those with learning disabilities because learners with special needs often have more difficulties completing work than peers without disabilities (Rivera & Smith, 1997). To make homework sessions productive, researchers have important recommendations for all involved, including the following three suggestions (Rivera & Smith, 1997; Salend, 1998; Sousa, 2001; Vaughn et al., 2003; Warger, 2001; Wicks-Nelson & Israel, 2003). First, special and regular educators should join forces to make sure homework has been individualized to the learner's special needs. Additionally, teachers of adolescents need to coordinate homework assignments, so learners are not overwhelmed by the amount of homework (e.g., with six teachers giving homework each night) and/or the type of work required.

Second, families and schools should communicate regularly about work done at home. Family members need to understand the school's expectations surrounding homework, and teachers can make suggestions on how to help youngsters complete their homework without stress or failure.

Third, educators should make homework accommodations by making adjustments to the amount and type of work required of those with specific learning needs. Adjustments to homework can be made by reducing the amount, extending the due date, using alternative assessments, giving time at school to complete homework, modifying the presentation and/or response methods of tasks, and keeping homework tasks separate from unfinished class assignments.

It is helpful if schools create systems for learners to track their homework assignments. An assignment notebook to record tasks and comments from family members and teachers helps keep learners organized.

Teachers should teach learners with special needs study and organizational skills. Such skills as taking good notes, monitoring time on task, checking work, gathering needed materials, and developing a homework routine will lead to successfully completing homework.

For the parents it is important to understand that educators sometimes disagree about the type of homework that should be assigned to learners with special needs. Many in special education (Rivera & Smith, 1997; Vaughn et al., 2003) recommend using homework for practice of skills already mastered. Others in special education (O'Shea et al., 2001; Peterson & Hittie, 2003) suggest assigning homework that is creative or an extension of learning to avoid the boredom of drill and practice assignments. Still others (Salend, 2001) believe the type of homework should be dictated by the instructional purpose and by how learners acquired content knowledge. For example, if the classroom learning session had students digesting facts through rote memorization, then the homework should be a practice format. Utilizing the previous suggestions should make the homework issue less tense and more productive for families and schools.

Behavior

Another area that can cause conflict for families and schools is learners' behavior.

> Ms. Sanderson has just announced that students should take the next five minutes to finish their journal entries and go to the corner of the room for the daily class meeting. One student, Josh, doesn't wait. He jumps up, pushes his journal and pencil off his desk, and heads toward the back of the classroom, pulling classmates' papers to the floor and touching their heads as he passes their desks. (Ayres & Hedeen, 1996, p.48)

Frequently when student behavior becomes disruptive to learning and dangerous to peers and adults, educators take drastic and reactive steps to expel students with disabilities from schools. Since IDEA 1997 has a stay-put provision, students can no longer be suspended from school for more than 10 days for exhibiting symptoms of their disability. This 10 day period must be used to determine if a long-term suspension or a movement to a more restrictive learning environment is warranted. Furthermore, the suspension policy has to apply to all students. If a long-term suspension is chosen, it can be no longer than 45 days and must apply to the total population of students. With long-term suspensions, an alternative education must be provided (Essex, 2002; Zurkowski, Kelly, & Griswold, 1998).

Individuals with social or emotional difficulties often exhibit behaviors that cause families and teachers extreme stress and frustration. In the classroom, teachers become exasperated when the learning environment is continually being disrupted (Anstine- Templeton, 2003). Families become tired of having to continually argue with children to get them to comply (Curran, 1999). Often, under such duress, adults may use counter productive coping skills and blame each other for the situation at school or home. Ayres and Hedeen (1996) state, "Often the best way to help students with behavior difficulties is to demonstrate flexibility and respect," and they offer four suggestions (p.48). First, adults might use a team approach to educate those with behavior problems. Family members and educators can work together, sharing ideas and creating an individualized plan that is consistently used by all. This way the youngster will not be able to "split" adults or play one against the other. Second, adults should create a shared vision or set of goals for the child or youth. These goals must focus on the expected, positive behavior. Third, adults must understand that inappropriate behaviors are communication that youngsters use to get their point across or to get their needs met. Adults need to determine what message or need is behind the disruptive behavior and teach more positive alternatives. Forth, adults ought to look beyond the inappropriate behavior and develop a preventive plan that helps the youngster communicate desires before he or she acts out. For example, rather than throwing the math book in frustration, the student can ask his peer tutor for help. In addition, at home give the child a timer that has been set 30 minutes prior to bedtime to avoid the arguing and whining that usually happens.

Often children with behavior problems want a sense of control in their home and school environments. The trick is to allow young people choices at home and in school, while at the same time, teaching how to use coping skills.

Medication

Whether or not the learner should or should not take medication can be another source of conflict between families and schools. Wicks-Nelson and Israel (2003) note that "the beliefs and attitudes that parents hold about their offspring's using medications for [social and emotional] problems is a crucial factor in whether medication will be accepted or rejected" (p.260).

Currently, medication is not recommended for those who have academic learning difficulties, unless the learner has a second disability that requires a prescription. Drug treatment is most often prescribed for learners who have social and emotional disabilities. Much controversy surrounds the use of drugs to enhance learning and control behavior of children and youth with disabilities (Kauffman, 2001; Rivera & Smith, 1997; Vaughn et al., 2003; Wicks-Nelson & Israel, 2003).

Medications for the treatment of ADHD have been the most controversial because they are usually stimulant drugs with known negative side effects and unknown long-term impacts. The most commonly use stimulants include Ritalin®, Dexedrine, Adderall, and Cylert. For ADHD, Ritalin® is the most frequently prescribed drug for children whereas Cylert is used for adolescents. Concerta is a new time-released form that requires only one dose per day (Vaughn et al., 2003). Possible side effects of stimulant medication include loss of appetite, stomach pains, headaches, irritability, sleep problems, mood changes, and jumpiness. A more serious side effect is motor and vocal tics; in which case, it is recommended to discontinue use (Wicks-Nelson & Israel, 2003). True long-term impacts have not been strongly documented; however, effects on physical growth, future drug abuse, and social immaturity are presently being investigated (Kauffman, 2001).

Many parents concerned about the growth, health, and emotional maturity of their children are cautious when it comes to drug treatment. Another concern families and critics voice is that the medication is overused because it is seen as a cure-all and/or is easy to obtain and dispense (Wicks-Nelson & Israel, 2003). Conversely, most teachers seeing the benefits on learning are strong supporters of medication, if it helps students focus, decreases anxiety, and improves inner calm (Vaughn et al., 2003). Proponents of medication (Kauffman, 2001) note that with the correct dosage, 90 percent of learners with ADHD are more teachable. Other social difficulties like aggression and anti-social behaviors are most often treated with a mood stabilizer, such as lithium (Wicks-Nelson & Israel, 2003). The use of these drugs is controversial because little research has been done on long-term side effects.

For emotional learning difficulties such as anxiety disorders, medication is not often the first choice of treatment. Psychological interventions are recommended as the initial treatment, with medication if needed. For obsessive-compulsive behavior, Prozac, Zoloft, Paxil, and Luvox can lessen symptoms. For childhood depression, antidepressants are prescribed, but their use is controversial because drug development research has been for adults, so impacts on children and youth are not known.

The following guidelines should help relieve the tensions surrounding the decision to use medication (Hartmann, 1993; Kauffman, 2001; Vaughn et al., 2003; Wicks-Nelson & Israel, 2003). First, parental beliefs need to be taken seriously and included in any discussion about treatments. If families are opposed to medication, then alternative treatments such as herbal, homeopathic, and neurofeedback therapies should be considered. Second, if medication is used, it should only be one component of the total treatment plan. Families, schools, physicians, and counselors should create well-rounded plans that include behavioral interventions (parent training as well as classroom organization and management), community treatment (psychologist or physician), and medication. Third, when medication is given, families and educators need to monitor the effects on their child's behavior and learning, so that the best dosage is determined.

CONCLUSION

Children with academic, social, and emotional learning difficulties feel different and isolated from their peers (Floss, 2001). These feelings of alienation are frequently magnified when families and educators are at odds with each other. Kids may secretly think that if they were not so stupid or weird, their family and teachers would not be fighting (Anstine-Templeton, 2003). Additionally, stress is common when living with and educating youngsters with learning disabilities. These tensions can be minimized if adults will listen to one another, show empathy for each other's situation, and always focus on what is best for the child. When educators, families, and communities come together to form true partnerships, they will discover their needs are remarkably similar. Both families and educators require respect, appreciation, information, and understanding. They want to have their efforts acknowledged. Most of all, they should support each other and look for the best in each other, so they can give that best to their children (Faber et al., 1996, p. 241).

Using a collaborative approach, school-family-community partnerships, can be developed to improve the self-confidence, academic abilities, social skills, and emotional well-being of students with learning disabilities.

TYPES OF LEARNING DISABILITIES CHART

Academic

Specific Learning Disabilities (LD)
- LD types include dyslexia (problems learning to read,) *dysgraphia* (problems learning to write), and *dyscalculia* (problems learning math).
- Constitutes the largest population of learning disabled children.
- Difficulties with academic learning but appear to have normal intellectual functioning.
- No known cause but genetic, organic, and environmental factors are being investigated. Individuals identified with LD have increased 150 percent in past decade. Affects more males than females.
- Students are overwhelmed, frustrated, and disorganized in new learning situations, have problems understanding and following directions, have trouble with visual or auditory perception, exhibit problems in writing, note taking, homework, tests, and/or have poor self-concept as learners.
- Students may exhibit behavior that mimics a learning disability but may only be a delay in maturation.
  (Kirk, 1963; Mastropieri & Scruggs, 2000; Peterson & Hittie, 2003; Sousa, 2001; Sturomski, 1997)

Nonverbal Learning Disabilities (NLD)
- Nonverbal information is impeded due to abnormal neurology. No known cause. Difficult to diagnose.

- Students lack ideas and knowledge necessary for daily social interactions and specific types of learning.
- Prevalence is increasing. More common in girls than boys.
- May include difficulty with visual-spatial organization, perception, and imaging.
- May include difficulty understanding connections between independent factors and relating these to the whole.
- May include difficulty understanding humor, multiple meanings of words, and nuances of language.
- May include lack of coordination and small motor skills related to handwriting.
- May include lack of social understanding.
- May include rigid behavior as well as difficulty with novelty and transition.
- Student at high risk for anxiety disorder, panic attack, obsessive-compulsive disorder, and, at times, suicide.
- May be extremely capable verbally, have excellent receptive language skills, and have strong literacy skills.
- Student can be very difficult to live with and teach.
- Parents and teachers may believe the child is intentionally controlling, stubborn, strong-willed, or emotionally disturbed.
(Matte & Bolaski, 1998; Rourke, 1995; Sheely, 2000; Thompson, 1997; Vacca, 2001; Wright, Bowen, & Zecker, 2000)

Gifted with Learning Disabilities
- May be one of the most under-identified and under-served groups of children with special learning needs. Statistics and data are lacking.
- Students are high-ability underachievers and may be faced with teachers who doubt they are gifted or bright, who believe they do not need help.
- Super sensitive, have difficulty dealing with change, loss, relationships, and developmental transitions such as entering school or a new school level.
- Perfectionist, highly critical of self and others, continually feel pressure, too focused on end product, may not enjoy the process.
- Unreasonable self-expectations, deep sense of justice, idealism, and empathy, may struggle with existential questions and theological concerns.
- May have difficulties with sequential tasks, memorization, computation, phonics, spelling, and organization.
- Tend to be underachievers, with low self-image, poor work habits, and negative attitudes toward academic tasks.
(Mastropieri & Scruggs, 2000; McCluskey & Trefinger, 1998; Peterson & Hittie, 2003; Sousa, 2001; Vaughn et al., 2003; Willard-Holt, 1999).

Social

Attention Deficit Hyperactivity Disorder (ADHD)

- Inattentive, hyperactive, and impulsive behaviors.
- Causes unknown, neurology suspected.
- For diagnosis, inattention and hyperactivity must be present before the age of 7, for more than 6 months, and in at least two environments (i.e., home and school).
- Affects about 4.1 percent of youth who are age 9 to 17, and 2 to 3 times more prevalent in boys than girls.
- May include short attention span and distractibility or the inability to concentrate for long periods of time.
- May include acting before thinking, causing severe problems.
- Hyperactivity or the inability to control motor activity affects less than 30 percent of children with ADHD. A hyperactive student moves from one task to another with little or no purpose.
- Unrelated ideas continually enter the student's mind distracting him or her from concentrating on tasks.
- Poor organizational skills cause problems in the multi-task environment of middle and high school.
- Younger students may have insatiability or unquenchable desire.
- May include social immaturity.
- Performance inconsistency is occasionally present.
- Some students are not able to tolerate change.
- Emotional state may change quickly (laughing, crying, anger, and depression).
- Poor short-term memory.
- Many preschool children diagnosed with ADHD may only have the symptoms which mimic the disorder.
- Only 50 percent those diagnosed with ADHD at age 4 will continue to have the symptoms in later childhood.
- Evaluation for ADHD must be a multi-step and multi-disciplinary procedure, in which information is gathered from a variety of sources including health, home, school, and community environments.
  (American Psychiatric Association, 2000; Moss & Dunlap, 1990; Sousa, 2001; Tannock & Martinussen, 2001; Vaughn et al., 2003; Sousa, 2001; Wicks-Nelson & Israel, 2003)

Conduct Disorder (CD)

- Genetics and other biological factors may contribute to CD, but it is believed that aggression is a learned behavior.
- Student may act out emotions and impulses toward others in aggressive and destructive ways.

- Aggression toward people and animals, including hitting, fighting, throwing objects, cruelty, and bullying.
- May include destruction of property, destroying belongings of others, and setting fires.
- May include stealing, lying, and burglary, truancy, and running away.
- To be diagnosed with CD, individuals must display three or more of the characteristics listed above, within the past 12 months, and be under the age of 18.
(American Psychiatric Association, 2000; Kauffman, 2001; Sousa, 2001; Wicks-Nelson & Israel, 2003)

Oppositional Defiant Disorder (ODD)

- If a child's problem behaviors do not meet the criteria for CD (not mean or cruel), but involve a pattern of defiant, angry, antagonistic, hostile, irritable, or vindictive behavior, ODD may be diagnosed. These children may blame others for their problems.
- Negativistic, hostile, and defiant behavior lasting at least six months, during which four or more of the following are present and frequent: loses temper, argues with adults, actively defies or refuses to comply with adults' requests or rules, deliberately annoys people, blames others for his or her mistakes or misbehavior, touchy or easily annoyed by others, angry and resentful, spiteful or vindictive.
- The disturbance in behavior causes significant problems in school and in relationships with family and friends.
(American Psychiatric Association, 2000)

Antisocial Behavior

- Sometimes known as "socialized aggression."
- Cause is closely linked to the student's environment.
- Characterized by covert deeds, rather than overt actions.
- Includes acts of delinquency, such as stealing, lying, running away, substance abuse, and gang activity.
- Estimated to be 4 to 10 percent and rising.
(Kauffman, 2001; Vaughn et al., 2003)

Emotional

Anxiety Disorders

- Anxiety is excessive tension, distress, and nervousness that comes with fears and worries about individuals, situations, and objects.
- Anxiety and fears can grow to be so chronic and unrelenting that they interfere with daily routines.

- Can be learned and/or due to genetic factors.
- Social Phobia Type is characterized by fear of interacting with peers and others.
- Specific Phobias is characterized by fear of an object or situation that leads to avoidance behavior.
- Generalized Anxiety Disorder (GAD) is characterized by excessive worry and fearful behavior for unfounded reasons.
- Obsessive-Compulsive Disorder (OCD)is a pattern of persistent thoughts and repetitive behaviors that are intrusive and unwanted, found more often in adolescents, rather than children.
- Post-Traumatic Stress Disorder (PTSD) is the result of witnessing distressing events, such as natural disasters and violence, characterized by nightmares, anger, and irritability are common symptoms.
- Panic Disorder is characterized by unexpected panic attacks, persistent concern about further attacks, and worry about what the attacks mean.
(Faber et al., 1996; Kauffman, 2001; Long & Morse, 1996; Sousa, 2001; Wicks-Nelson & Israel, 2003)

Mood Disorders
- Major depression is diagnosed when a student cannot, study, sleep, eat, or enjoy once pleasurable activities. Characterized by persistent sad mood, irritability, loss of interest, lack of sleep, decreased appetite, lack of energy, motor agitation, difficulty concentrating, feeling of worthlessness or guilt, and continual thoughts about death and suicide. It is estimated that 6 percent of children ages 9 to 17 have major depression and that the onset of depression is occurring earlier in life. The cause of depression is unknown but environmental and genetic influences are strongly suspected.
- Dysthymia is characterized by long-term, chronic depression that is not disabling, but keeps one from functioning or feeling well. Students may also experience major depressive episodes at some time in their lives.
- Bipolar Disorder, also called manic-depressive illness, is characterized by cycling mood changes from severe highs (mania) and lows (depression). Cycling is usually slow but can be rapid. When in the depression cycle, the student may have all the symptoms of major depression. When in the manic cycle, the students has too much energy and may behave in ways that causes serious problems. Mania, left untreated, may worsen to a psychotic state.
(American Psychiatric Association, 2000; Kauffman, 2001; Long & Morse, 1996; National Institute of Mental Health, 2000; Sousa, 2001; Wicks-Nelson & Israel, 2003)

REFERENCES

American Psychiatric Association. (2000). *Diagnostic and Statistical Manual of Mental Disorders, Text Revision* (4th Ed.). Washington, DC: Author.

Anstine-Templeton, R. (1995). ADHD: A teachers' guide [Monograph]. *The Oregon Conference Monograph, 7,* 43-52. Eugene: University of Oregon.

Anstine-Templeton, R. (2003). *When kids get angry: What parents and teachers can do.* Unpublished manuscript, Ferris State University, Big Rapids, MI.

Ayres, B. J., & Hedeen, D. L. (1996). Been there, done that, didn't work: Alternative solutions for behavior problems. *Educational Leadership, 53*(5). Retrieved July 22, 2003, from the Association for Supervision and Curriculum Development website http://www.ascd.org/readingroom/edlead/9602/ayres.html

Clayton, M. D., & Forton, M. B. (2001). *Classroom spaces that work.* Greenfield, MA: Northeast Foundation for Children.

Curran, D. (1999). *Tired of arguing with your kids?* Notre Dame, IN: Sorin Books.

Davern, L. (1996). Listening to parent of children with disabilities. *Educational Leadership, 53*(7), 61-63.

Dettmer, P., Thurston, L. P., & Dyck, N. (2002). *Consultation, collaboration, and teamwork for students with special needs.* Boston, MA: Allyn & Bacon.

Essex, N. L. (2002). *School law and the public schools: A practical guide for educational leaders* (2nd Ed.). Boston: Allyn & Bacon.

Faber, A., Mazlish, E., Nyberg, L., & Anstine-Templeton, R. (1996). *How to talk so kids can learn at home and in school.* New York: Simon & Schuster.

Floss, J. M. (2001). *Nonverbal learning disability: How to recognize it and minimize its effects* (Report No. EDO-EC-01-14). Arlington, VA: The Council for Exceptional Children. (ERIC Document Reproduction Service No. ED461238)

Hartmann, T. (1993). *Attention deficit disorder: A different perception.* Lancaster, PA. Underwood-Miller.

Haury, D. L., & Milbourne, L. A. (1999). *Helping your child with science* (Report No. EDO-SE-99-01). Columbus, OH: ERIC Clearinghouse for Science, Mathematics, and Environmental Education. (ERIC Document Reproduction Service No. ED432447)

Hulsebosch, P., & Logan, L. (1998). Breaking it up or breaking it down: Inner-City parents as co-constructors of school improvement. *Educational Horizons, 77*(1), 30-36.

Individuals with Disabilities Education Act. (1997, March 12). Assistance to States for the Education of Children with Disabilities and the Early Intervention Program for Infants and Toddlers with Disabilities. 34 C.F.R., 300 & 303. Vol. 64, No. 48.

Jones, V., & Jones, L. (in press). *Comprehensive classroom management: Creating communities of support and solving problems* (7th Ed.). Boston: Allyn & Bacon.

Kauffman, J. M. (2001). *Characteristics of emotional and behavioral disorders of children and youth.* (7th Ed.). Upper Saddle, NJ: Prentice Hall.

Knoblauch, B., & McLane, K. (1999). *Rights and responsibilities of parents of children with disabilities* (Report No. EDO-EC-99-3). Reston, VA: The Council for Exceptional Children. (ERIC Document Reproduction Service No. ED437766)

Long, N. J., & Morse, W. C. (1996). *Conflict in the classroom: The education of at-risk and troubled students.* Austin, TX: ProEd.

Mastropieri, M. A., & Scruggs, T. E. (2000). *The Inclusive Classroom Strategies for Effective Instruction.* Upper Saddle River, NJ: Prentice Hall.

Matte, R. R., & Bolaski, J. A. (1998). Nonverbal learning disabilities: An overview. *Intervention in School and Clinic, 34*(1), 39-42.

McCluskey, K. W., & Treffinger, D. J. (1998). Nurturing talented but troubled children and youth. *Reclaiming Children and Youth, 6*(4), 215-219.

Moss, R. A., & Dunlap, H. H. (1990). *Why Johnny can't concentrate: Coping with attention deficit problems.* New York: Bantam Books.

National Institute of Mental Health. (2000). *Depression in children and adolescents: A fact sheet for physicians.* Retrieved July 22, 2003, from the NIMH website http://www.nimh.nih.gov/publicat/depchildresfact.cfm

O'Shea, D. J., O'Shea, L. J., Algozzine, R., & Hammitte, D. J. (2001). *Families and teachers of individuals with disabilities: Collaborative orientations and responsive practices.* Boston: Allyn & Bacon.

Peterson, J. S. (2001). Successful adults who were once adolescent underachievers. *Gifted Child Quarterly 45*(4), 236-250.

Peterson, J. M., & Hittie, M. M. (2003). *Inclusive teaching: Creating effective schools for all learners.* Boston: Allyn & Bacon.

Rich, D. (1998). Reaching the family: How teachers build the policy bridge. *Educational Horizons, 76*(2), 77-80.

Rivera, D. P., & Smith, D. D. (1997). *Teaching students with learning and behavior problems* (3rd Ed.). Boston: Allyn & Bacon.

Robinson, E. L., & Fine, M. J. (1994). Developing collaborative home-school relationships. *Preventing School Failure, 39*(1), 9-15.

Rourke, B. P. (1995). *Syndrome of nonverbal learning disabilities.* New York: Guilford Press.

Salend, S. J. (1998). *Effective mainstreaming: Creating inclusive classrooms* (3rd Ed.). New Paltz, NY: Merrill.

Salend, S. J. (2001) *Creating inclusive classrooms: Effective and reflective practices* (4th Ed.). Upper Saddle River, NJ: Merrill/Prentice Hall.

Sheely, R. (2000, Summer). Nonverbal learning disorder: A closer look. *The Source, 1,* 6.

Sousa, D. A. (2001). *How the special needs brain learns.* Thousand Oaks, CA: Corwin Press.

Sturomski, N. (1997). Teaching students with learning disabilities to use learning strategies. *NICHCY News Digest, 25,* 2-12.

Tannock, R., & Martinussen, R. (2001). Reconceptualizing ADHD. *Educational Leadership, 59*(3), 20-25.

Thompson, S. (1997). *The source for nonverbal learning difficulties.* East Moline, IL: LinguiSystems.

Vacca, D. M. (2001). Confronting the puzzle of nonverbal learning disabilities. *Educational Leadership, 59*(3), 26-31.

Vaughn, S., Bos, C. S., & Schumm, J. S. (2003). *Teaching exceptional, diverse, and at-risk students in the general education classroom.* Boston: Allyn & Bacon.

Warger, C. (2001). *Five homework strategies for teaching students with disabilities* (Report No. EDO-EC-01-3). Arlington, VA: The Council for Exceptional Children. (ERIC Document Reproduction Service No. ED452628)

Wicks-Nelson, R., & Israel, A. C. (2003). *Behavior disorders of childhood* (5th Ed.). Upper Saddle, NJ: Prentice Hall.

Willard-Holt, C. (1999). *Dual exceptionalities* (Report No. EDO-99-2). Reston, VA: The Council for Exceptional Children. (ERIC Document Reproduction Service No. ED430344)

Wright, B. A., Bowen, R. W., & Zecker, S. G. (2000). Nonlinguistic perceptual deficits associated with reading and language disorders. *Current Opinion in Neurobiology, 10*, 482-486.

Zurkowski, J. K., Kelly, P. S., & Griswold, D. E. (1998). Discipline and IDEA 1997: Instituting a new balance. *Intervention in School and Clinic, 34*(1), 3-9.

CHAPTER 6

SCHOOLS AND FAMILIES OF STUDENTS WITH AN EMOTIONAL DISTURBANCE
Allies and Partners

Carl I. Fertman

John's disruptive, aggressive, and oppositional behaviors were well known by the Principals of the high school he attended. At the start of the school year the social worker at school asked his mother to come in for a meeting. John's mother worked two jobs and was unable to attend a meeting. John's father traveled much of the time and was also unavailable. It was a difficult situation. His parents didn't want any more bad behavior reports about John. However, we also knew that without help and support from his family, John would only go downhill. Turning around John's behavior meant partnering with his family, getting to know what support they needed and helping them to meet these needs. We did it. The school helped John's family access mental health services and together the school, family and his mental health provider collaborated to develop plans to get John back on track. This year John has had improved academic success and less discipline referrals than in previous years.

Promising Practices Connecting Schools to Families of Children with Special Needs, pages 79–99.
A Volume in: Family School Community Partnership Issues
Copyright © 2004 by Information Age Publishing, Inc.
All rights of reproduction in any form reserved.
ISBN: 1-930608-99-3 (hardcover), 1-930608-98-5 (paperback)

INTRODUCTION

Students with an emotional disturbance often have great difficulty relating appropriately to adults and peers. Disturbance in mood, development and behavior can qualify a student for support services for an emotional disturbance. These students often exhibit difficulty problem solving, expressing emotion, and often react inappropriately to redirection or failure. Students with behavior disorders often have difficulty accepting responsibility for misbehavior, are aggressive and have histories of fighting and disobedience in their school and communities. These students are usually the most challenging for teachers. Their problems are severe, pervasive, and chronic, rather than minor, situational, or transitory. Many students with an emotional disturbance are removed from the regular classroom because of their consistently disruptive behavior (Kauffman, Lloyd, Baker, & Riedel, 1995). Because these students are so challenging, schools cannot meet all their needs alone. School personnel who work with these students must gain the support and trust of the parents of these students and help them access support services in their community when necessary. School personnel, parents, and support services must collaborate to plan consistent interventions designed to modify and ameliorate negative behaviors for these students to achieve academic success.

Sadly, students with a serious emotional disturbance have many negative educational outcomes (U.S. Department of Education, 1998). They fail more classes, miss more days of school, have lower grades, are retained at the same grade level more often than other students with other disability labels, and drop out more frequently than any other group of students. The poor outcomes reflect the fact that many students with an emotional disturbance and their families do not have access to a full continuum of mental health and support services within the school system and local community. Many youth with an emotional disturbance and their families rarely get the kind of help they need at the time they need it. Services and supports are fragmented, isolated, and rigid. Most students receive services in environments that separate them from their peers, such as special education classes, day schools, hospitals, home, and residential facilities. While those students who are placed in mainstream classrooms rarely receive the supports that they need to succeed (U.S. Department of Education, 1998).

Caring families, schools, and communities working together can help children and adolescents with an emotional disturbance. A broad range of services is often necessary to meet the needs of these young people and families. However the provision of proper services to these students and families is a complex and challenging process for all involved, and many youth fall through the cracks, failing to receive the education or support services they need. Approaches for schools to involve families of children and adolescents with an emotional disturbance in order to improve students' social, emotional, academic, and vocational outcomes are the focus of this chapter.

IMPORTANCE OF FAMILY INVOLVEMENT

In 1994 with the publication of the National Agenda for Achieving Better Results for Children and Youth with Serious Emotional Disturbance (U.S. Department of Education), parents and family were recognized as allies with valuable knowledge to contribute to schools and their child's academic, social, emotional, and vocational outcomes. The National Agenda changed what it meant for schools to involve family members of students with an emotional disturbance. Traditionally, parent involvement was engaging parents in ongoing teacher communications, parents volunteering in the school, helping a child with homework, and reading aloud. As a result of the National Agenda, parent involvement changed and expanded. The objective is now for family members to have the resources and support to participate on community interagency teams, to assist in the design, implementation, and evaluation of services and curriculum. Family members became advocates for research initiatives focused on children and families and helped to make policy at the local, state, and national level (Osher & Osher, 2002).

At schools, family members of youth presenting emotional and behavior problems, can facilitate positive educational and mental health outcomes by providing comprehensive information about the child's health and development, social and educational history, and learning and coping styles. Parents can enact changes in the home environment to enhance the child's well-being and monitor the effectiveness of educational and therapeutic interventions. Family involvement can ensure that schools and community programs adequately meet the needs of the students and families that they serve, and empower families to take a central role in their children's social, educational, and emotional development (Bickham, Pizarro, Warner, Rosenthal, & Weist, 1998; Wagner, 1995).

Family involvement can facilitate family members learning new skills, becoming knowledgeable about school, and communicating more thoroughly with teachers. Empowered family members may accomplish more meaningful goals for themselves and their children. They are able to build their capacity to advocate for their children, act with confidence on their own behalf, and give greater levels of support to other parents (Cheney & Osher, 1997; Koren & DeChillo, 1995).

CHALLENGES TO FAMILY INVOLVEMENT

Involving families of students with an emotional disturbance in schools is often difficult. The challenges stem from the multiple perspectives of those who hold a stake in meeting the needs of the students and their families. Families, students, mental health professionals, and school teachers, principals, social workers, and counselors all have differing ideas about how and what it means to involve families in schools. Family members who interact with their child's school frequently report feeling marginalized and feeling as if they are perceived as uncaring or too overwhelmed in their own lives to be an effective parent. Families often feel exhausted, shamed, isolated and a lacking support.

Many students with an emotional disturbance have families who struggle with multiple stressors, including poverty, single parenting, joblessness, racism, violence, drug abuse, alcoholism, and their own mental health issues. Parents own mental health and life concerns can impair their parenting abilities. Misconceptions about the roles of school systems and mental health services can cause additional confusion (Federation of Families for Children's Mental Health, 2001). Some parents themselves have had problems in school, and may avoid working with school personnel due to painful memories of these problems (Harry, 1992).

Families often have concerns about maintaining a sense of control over parenting their children. Professional jargon used by both educators and mental health professionals can be perceived as condescending and cause parents to feel ineffective in addressing their concerns about their own children. Family members may fear that they will be blamed for a teenager's problems. In addition, many, if not most families, view school and mental health issues and services with suspicion and stigma, and have concerns about the confidentiality of information shared with school and mental health professionals. Such negative perceptions perpetuate negative school and family relationships.

Students, particularly adolescents, are adept at keeping parents and teachers at odds. They are establishing independence and autonomy and may not want family members involved in their school and mental health treatment. A variety of factors may influence students' willingness to involve their families with their school. Family members may not approve of the child's behavior in school. Students want to conceal the problems (e.g. disruptive behavior, sexuality, substance abuse) that are apparent to school personnel. This is especially true when there is potential for volatile family reaction, family conflict, or abuse (Bickham, Pizarro, Warner, Rosenthal, & Weist, 1998).

Additional challenges to family involvement may be created by administrative structures and problems associated with service systems and schools. The social service community, including schools, has often used the challenging nature of the symptoms and many of the issues that these families face to place blame onto parents and other family members for their children's behavior (DeChillo, Koren, & Mezera, 1996). Just the sheer number of professional adults involved with their child can seem overwhelming and intimidating to parents. While mental health treatment is available, it is often difficult for families to access. It can be expensive and time consuming. Community mental health programs may lack the resources (e.g. funding, staffing) to provide families with evening and weekend appointments, child care, and transportation. Programs also may lack resources to provide the training and support needed by clinicians to facilitate family involvement. Students often require services from several sources. Parents are challenged to coordinate services and activities. They may encounter conflicting requirements, different atmospheres and expectations, and contradictory messages. Furthermore, as schools strive to meet the needs of these children, many teachers and support staff are cast in unfamiliar roles and acquire new responsibilities with little preparation and support. Low teacher expectations for students with an emotional disturbance reinforce their generally poor performance in schools, and such students have been pushed out of their local schools by transfer, suspension, and hostility (Osher & Osher, 1995; Rumberger & Larson, 1994).

Another way to view the challenges is at a more personal level. Family members and school professionals have different roles in the life of a child that need consideration (Cheney & Osher, 1997; Getzels, 1974; Katz, 1984; Keyes, 2002). A framework developed by Katz (1984) explores the differences in roles between the family (parenting) and school (teaching). In the model, the teacher's (school) role is specific to schooling, while the family involvement is universal in all aspects of the child's life. Traditionally, teachers and schools are responsible for all the children for a specific period confined to the school setting, and therefore the teacher's role is more objective, detached, and rational, using insight, techniques, and abilities to support each child. The professional role is shaped by professional knowledge about all children. Parental relationships, on the other hand are shaped by their own child for whom they are responsible 24 hours a day. They are likely to demonstrate intense partiality, attachment, and even irrationality in their interactions about their own child (Keyes, 2002; Katz 1984). An educator, B. Huff (personal communication, January 30, 2003), made the point that the range of emotions and behavior of these parents in light of the intensity of the parenting role is broad and can be anticipated. However, all too often, given the difference in perspectives and roles in a child's life, a danger exists to unfairly label parents as unfriendly, bad, and uncooperative, while the schools and community agency staff are perceived by educators as good and correct. Sometimes the parents are simply having a normal reaction to a difficult situation. The challenge for school personnel is not to be overwhelmed or pushed away by the family members' emotions, which potentially might derail the family involve-

TABLE 1
Distinctions Between Family and Schools in Their
Central Tendencies on Seven Role Dimensions

Role Dimension	Family (parenting)	School (teaching)
1. Scope of function	Diffuse and limitless	Specific and limited
2. Intensity of affect	High	Low
3. Attachment	Optimum attachment	Optimum detachment
4. Rationality	Optimum irrationality	Optimum rationality
5. Spontaneity	Optimum spontaneity	Optimum intentionality
6. Partiality	Partial	Impartial
7. Scope of responsibility	Individual	Whole group

ment. The challenge is to be accepting and supportive of the family members' emotional states while helping to guide and partner with then to address the students' needs. Table 1 provides a look into the contrasting focus of educators and family which might facilitate this understanding (Katz, 1984; Keyes, 2002).

In summary, recognizing the multiple perspectives of those who hold a stake in meeting the needs of students with emotional disturbance and the roles of families and schools in the lives of the student sets a framework to examine family school involvement strategies that work.

FAMILY INVOLVEMENT STRATEGIES

Five major school and family involvement approaches are used in schools to partner and collaborate with families. Although they would be effective for all parents and families, as currently discussed they are for families who have a child or teenager who has meet the criteria to receive special education services due to an emotional disturbance. The five approaches are the following:

a. forming helping relationships,
b. creating family friendly schools,
c. family school provider collaborations,
d. family network organizations, and
e. parent and family education.

The purpose of each approach is for the school and family to be allies and partners to address barriers to student and family achievement and success.

Under the Individual with Disabilities Education Act (IDEA), a child or adolescent with an emotional disturbance requires a plan of care based on the severity and duration of symptoms. Optimally, this plan is developed with the family, service providers, and a service coordinator who is referred to as a case manager. Whenever possible, the child or adolescent is involved in decisions. Tying together all the various supports and services in a plan of care for a particular child and family is commonly referred to as a *system of care* (Stroul & Friedman, 1986). A system of care is designed to improve the child's ability to function in all areas of life: at home, at school, and in the community.

Of all the organizations and services involved in the system of care, the school is accountable by law (IDEA) to service provision. Schools must develop an Individual Education Plan (IEP) in concert with a parent or guardian. Although other providers and organizations may also participate in the development of the IEP, the school bears the burden and opportunity of the IDEA mandate. Therefore, it is teachers, counselors, special educators, and administrators who work with families to address the educational needs of students with an emotional disturbance.

HELPING RELATIONSHIPS

Fundamental to family involvement is a good relationship between families and schools. Without underlying trust and honesty between school professionals and family members, there can be no expectations for positive outcomes for anyone: student, family, or school. Of all the places where children and adolescents with an emotional disturbance spend time, schools are where many families feel their children and adolescents are the most vulnerable. Family members say their relationship with school personnel make or break their willingness to be involved in school. And while families and schools recognize the value of collaborating and working together, the reality of the relationships can be frustrating for everyone involved.

Forming helping relationships with family members as individuals allows you to establish connections with family members separate from their child and separate from the IEP process. The first step in forming the relationship is to recognize and validate the level at which families are already involved with their children. In most cases they live with the child or teenager whose behavior may be out of control and troubled. The daily living can be exhausting. Without the school professionals' acceptance and knowledge of the current level of the child or adolescent's involvement in their own family, getting family members to be involved with school partnerships is not realistic. Be aware that as the student moves through the school system, parents must adjust to new faces, attitudes, and the culture of a new school. They will bring with them their history with the school district. These changes should be recognized and validated. We need to get to know the family members as people who bring personal histories and resources to the relationship.

Education professionals (e.g. teachers, school nurses, counselors, social workers administrators) and family members each bring different perspectives and experiences to their relations (Figure 1; Keyes, 2002; Woodside & McClam, 2002). Both the professionals and family members bring attitudes, values, feelings, communication skills, experiences, culture, roles, sense of efficacy, and personality, which may be similar or may be very different. In addition, the family members bring knowledge of their child, needs, problems, and expectations about what will happen, whereas the school people come with professional training and skills and knowledge of all students, ideally to assist and support the family. In building helping relationships the focus must be on equality, listening, flexibility, sensitivity, and being available.

Relationship building takes time for families of children with an emotional disturbance. Over a period of weeks and months relationships between family members and school professionals grow and develop. The relationships are best viewed as long term, spanning the school years and beyond. Difficult periods with troubled student behavior are weathered, the disappointments of families and schools acknowledged. Better student behavior and outcomes are designed and agreed upon. However, rewarding and satisfying communications may or may not balance out the difficult periods. Meeting expectations and demands may sometimes be beyond the reach of both families and schools. Throughout these periods persistent and consistent communication between school professionals and parents is needed to build and maintain the relationships.

In an ideal world the relationships between schools and families would be conflict free and without failure. However, inevitably there are conflicts and failures in communication, hurt feelings, and unsatisfactory outcomes. Looking for opportunities to resolve conflict, with the use of problem solving and anger management strategies should be viewed as part of the relationship building process. Simply anticipating the conflicts, failures, hurts, and poor outcomes, is unsatisfactory without taking preventive action.

Matching families and school professionals is often random, but there is considerable evidence that compatibility between the two is important for effective relationships and working together. The following questions (Rogers, 1958; Woodside & McClam, 2002) may help you increase your self awareness in relation to your own relationship building skills with family members.

- Can I be perceived as trustworthy, dependable, and consistent?
- Can I express myself well enough that the family members understand what I am saying?

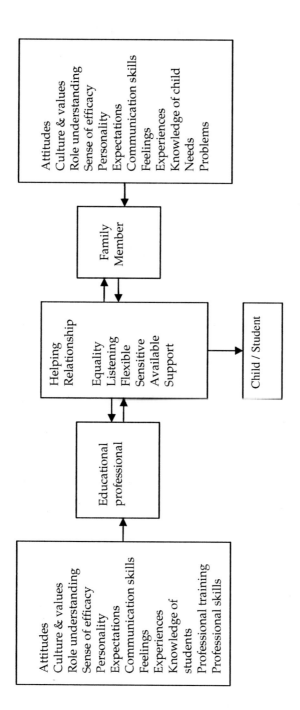

FIGURE 1

Helping Relationship with Family Member Focused on the Child/Student.

- Can I experience attitudes of warmth, caring, liking, interest, and respect for the family members?
- Can I separate my needs from those of the family members?
- Am I secure enough myself to allow the family members to be separate and independent of me?
- Am I able to see the world as the family members do?
- Can I accept the family members as they are?

In the process of building relationships with families, we need to look at what families bring and what the team of school professionals composed of teachers, counselors, nurses, psychologist, social workers, or school administrators bring to the partnership. Families are a rich source of information. They can provide an intimate knowledge and understanding of their child: their likes, hobbies, behaviors at home and community, the beliefs and the strengths of the family system. Families share a common language, and when school and parents agree on the behavior goals of the child, parents can monitor progress firsthand and support at home the same goals as the school. School and community professionals bring a body of knowledge and expertise about learning and mental health. Parents must be aware that school and community professionals abide by a code of ethics that set standards of acceptable personal and professional behavior such as confidentiality. To involve more parents and families in schools requires us to think in new ways about our relationships with them. Forming relationship will go a long way to create parent and school partnerships to support the success of students with an emotional disturbance.

FAMILY FRIENDLY SCHOOLS

Creating a school environment that is family friendly will also ease the tension and create the opportunity for schools and families to partner and collaborate to meet the needs of students with emotional disturbance. Parents, teachers, counselors, social workers, and principals in discussions have suggested strategies that lend support to efforts to build good school and family relationships (Bickham et al., 1998; Federation of Families for Children's Mental Health, 1999; Jordon, Orozco, & Averett, 2002):

- Be flexible and creative: It takes time to build relationship with parents and to involve them in meaningful activities and conversations. Providing flexibility in time to meet with parents, talking on the telephone, and having impromptu feedback sessions when parents and family members are available all help to build trust and rapport.
- Assess and respect the needs of the families: Assess the ongoing needs of the families. Regularly talk with the families individually and in small groups about their needs and goals.

- Provide resources for families: Make space for families and parents in the school. If we want parents to come, we have to take time to make them feel welcomed. Simple procedures of offering a beverage to drink and snack are helpful. Try to provide access to telephones and transportation if necessary.
- Establish a family feedback loop: We constantly want to be checking to ensure that the activities and services of the school and community are addressing the needs of the child or adolescent. Ask the parents, family members, and student directly about the services. Ask the community providers to assess the family's satisfaction with the services. Talk with the local family support organization about conducting a feedback and brainstorming session on how to improve services and service gaps.
- Give clear and consistent messages about mental health: Let students, parents, and family know that (a) every child's mental health is important, (b) many children have mental health problems, (c) these problems are real and painful and can be severe, (d) mental health problems can be recognized and treated, and (e) caring families and communities working together can help.
- Look for activities to involve families: School and community activities are places where teachers and families spend time together in a non-threatening environment. Sporting events, church gatherings, and holiday celebrations are all potentially common grounds. Invite families to class activities, send birthday and holiday greeting cards, and telephone when their child is doing well. These activities provide a means to have a shared experience and to be a part of the school and community that is not necessarily focused on the student. They can serve as a basis for more personal sharing of interests and emotions.
- Create a welcoming, culturally competent school: The disproportionate and inappropriate identification of culturally and linguistically diverse students as emotionally disturbed raises concerns of miscommunications and stereotyping. Recommended solutions are staff training, community outreach, culturally diverse staff, community liaisons recruited from the community, and respect for the diversity of the student population.

FAMILY-SCHOOL-PROVIDER COLLORABORATION

Family, school, and provider collaborations are a model to deliver services to students with an emotional disturbance and their families. They reflect an evolution in thinking about how best to serve students and their families. Their roots are firmly grounded in the National Agenda (U.S. Department of Education, 1994). The collaborations provide the linkage between parent, community support, and school to establish continuity of care. The services are family-centered, and are designed and delivered according to the particular needs and preferences of the family members. Plans are designed to build on strengths and resources, rather than weakness and deficits. Consensus is gathered from the group to determine the needs that are in the best interests of the child. Professionals and families are seen as equal partners. Educational and behavioral goals are agreed upon. Services are comprehensive and efforts are made to ensure that the services are accessible to the family and student. The concepts of equality, mutuality, and teamwork are terms used to describe the collaborations (Osher & Osher, 2002; Worthington, Hernandez, Friedman, & Uzzell, 2001).

Family-school-provider collaborations have flourished with the support of federal, state, and local funding. Federal funding for many of the partnerships comes from the Center for Mental Health Services, under the umbrella of the Substance Abuse and Mental Health Services Administration, which is part of the U.S. Department of Health and Human Services (Simpson, Koroloff, Friesen, & Gac, 1999; Woodruff, et al., 1999). An example of such a collaborative is the Community Connections for Families (CCF) implemented by the Allegheny County Department of Human Services beginning in October 1998 in five partner communities in Pittsburgh, Pennsylvania and surrounding communities (www.communityconnectionsforfamilies.org). At the heart of CCF is a strong family and community partnership that endeavors to bring families services and supports that they need, not simply what is dictated by traditional services, contracts, funding, and institutional structures. CCF is designed to support the following 12 core values (Table 2) seen as the foundation of successful colorations.

CCF's goal is to improve coordination and service integration by overcoming the system fragmentation that impacts children and youth with serious emotional disturbances and their families. Hence, CCF service coordinators work with all child-serving systems, including Children, Youth and Families (CYF), schools, juvenile justice, and mental health, to deliver a seamless, highly flexible array of service and support options to families. CCF takes pride in the fact that it serves the entire family, not only the child with an emotional disturbance. This is accomplished by empowering families and communities through activities such as support groups and educational opportunities, and by incorporating informal supports (such as cultural/spiritual supports, community memberships, etc.) into the service planning process.

Each of the five CCF communities employs a number of service coordinators and family support specialists depending on the communities' unique needs. These staff members connect families and their children to a wide range of services and supports. They help them gather the information they need, secure the best resources for their child, coordinate service

TABLE 2
Community Connections for Families Core Values

Value	*Practice*
Youth-Centered	Services and supports always ensure that the child's voice is heard and needs are being met.
Family Focused and Driven	Families participate in all planning and implementation of services and supports. The family's expertise is valued and respected. Services are provided in ways that enable, encourage and assist families in planning and implementation.
Safety (Youth, Family and Community)	Services and supports are developed and implemented to ensure the safety and well-being of the youth, family, and community.
Individualized	Each youth's and each family's culture, strengths, priorities and needs are unique. Therefore, services and supports are tailored to match and respond to each youth and family's particular situation.
Strengths-Based	Partnerships, services and supports reflect the identified strengths and needs of each youth and family. Strengths are continually assessed, appreciated, utilized and celebrated.
Community-Based/Least Restrictive	Services and supports are accessible and provided in the home community of the youth and family. Community Connections for Families actively cultivates community support and development of resources for youth and families. Every effort is made to keep the youth in their home or in the least restrictive environment.
Cultural Competency	Services and supports reflect the unique values, beliefs, traditions, preferences, and practices of the youth and family.
Relentless Advocacy	Advocacy is expressed by a community and system committing to a youth and family. No youth or family falls through the cracks. No one ever gives up on a youth or family.
Outcome-Based	Outcomes should be clear and measurable. They are used to guide the delivery and completion of services to youth and family and to develop and sustain Community Connections for Families.
Cost-Effective/Cost Responsible	Cost effective services and supports blend formal and informal resources which are continually reviewed to ensure responsible financial use. Community Connection for Families staff, families, and communities determine the expenditure of funds to best meet the needs of all program participants.
Education	All youth are entitled to an education that best meets their needs and utilizes their strengths.
Physical and Mental Well-Being	Services and supports ensure the best possible physical and emotional care based on the youth's and family's preferences and needs.

delivery among the systems in which their child is involved, and provide advocacy and emotional support. Listed below are the five major CCF services. All services administered by CCF are voluntary and free of charge.

- Service Coordination: The CCF service coordinator works with the child and family and their team to ensure that all necessary services to support them in their home and community are put into place.
- Child and Family Team and Service Plan: The CCF service coordinator and the family form a team of individuals to create and monitor a service and support plan tailored to the unique strengths and needs of the child. This plan guides how all services are provided. Teams are often made up of people from other child service systems that work with the family as well as other friends or family members identified by the family.
- Family Support Specialist: The CCF Family Support Specialist supports families by providing information, advocacy, and emotional support. They may also be part of the child and family team.
- Educational Opportunities: CCF offers several training and educational events for families county-wide.
- Support Groups: Each CCF partner community offers a support group for parents and youth with emotional disturbance.

Children enrolled in CCF must be between the ages of 6 and 14 years, have a diagnosis of a serious emotional disturbance , be involved in two or more child serving systems (e.g. mental health, schools, juvenile justice, child welfare/child protection services, mental retardation/developmental disabilities, or drug and alcohol), and live in one of the five partner communities.

FAMILY NETWORK ORGANIZATIONS

As the service delivery model for students with an emotional disturbance and their families shifted to student and family centered emphasis, organizations focused on family support and advocacy developed (Bryant-Comstock, Huff, & VanDenBerg, 1996). The major family network organization is the Federation of Families for Children's Mental Health (FFCMH) formed in 1989. Its purpose is to bolster family members' individual voices across states, to gather and disseminate information, and to collectively address the needs of families dealing with emotional, behavioral, and mental health issues across child and family serving systems. Families wanted their own access to information and they wanted to affect national level policy and the development of those policies within states.

Family participation and support in a system of care is fundamental to the FFCMH. Therefore, it works to develop and implement policies, legislation, funding mechanisms, and service delivery systems that utilize the strengths of families in the following ways:

- Ensuring that they are equal partners in planning, implementation, and evaluation of services.
- Viewing the child as a whole person and family as a whole unit rather than emphasizing the disability.
- Educating and empowering families and children to make decisions about their own lives.
- Encouraging innovative programming that increases options and promotes the integration of services.

A visit to the FFCMH website (www. ffcmh.org) links families to the federation's state and local affiliates, newsletter, technical assistance, and Parent Involved Network (PIN). Since 1989 the FFCMH has spun a national network of family network organizations. The state and local affiliates focus on establishing and strengthening family networks to provide family to family support and resources. The Federation newsletter, *Claiming Children*, provides parents and families practical actions and tips for working with schools, community providers, and mental health professionals. Likewise it gives parents information on advocacy and program evaluation. Technical assistance supports developing family leaders through peer to peer mentoring, typically offering advice and support by telephone. Family leaders are also developed at national meetings and through formal curricula. The PIN lets families and family - run organizations share policy changes occurring in their own states, both good and troubling developments. It also lets them seek advice and support and learn from one another's successes and failures.

Helping parents feel valued, supported, competent, and respected is the primary motivation for encouraging their participation in the state and local FFCMH. The organizations are parent-run advocacy groups. They can answer parents' questions and provide a network of individuals for brainstorming, problem solving, linkages, and services.

A number of other national and local organizations also provide families information, resources, support, access, and linkages to programs and services for their child or adolescent. The National Mental Health Association (www. nmha.org) is a consumer based advocacy group heavily committed to mental health rights and legislation. It is in the forefront of federal legislation on such topics as deinstitutionalization, the Child and Adolescent Service System Program (CASSP), and mental health insurance parity. The National Alliance for the Mentally Ill (NAMI) is a nonprofit, grassroots, self-help, support and advocacy organization of consumers, families, and friends of people with a severe emotional disturbance, such as schizophrenia, major depression, bipolar disorder, obsessive-compulsive disorder, and anxiety disorders. Working on the national, state, and local levels, NAMI provides education about severe brain disorders, supports increased funding for research, and advocates for adequate health insurance, housing, rehabilitation, and jobs for people with serious psychiatric illnesses. Consumers, family members, and friends are encouraged to contact NAMI on the web at www.nami.org or to call the toll-free NAMI HelpLine for information and referral to the NAMI affiliate group in their area. The NAMI HelpLine is staffed by trained volunteers Monday through Friday, 10:00 a.m. to 5:00 p.m. (Eastern time) and has a 24-hour, 7-day-a-week message line. The HelpLine number is 1-800-950-NAMI [6264].

At the most sophisticated level of family involvement organizations there are federally funded research and training centers focused on family support and children's mental health. Although for many families of a child or teenager with an emotional disturbance these organizations may be a reach, at the very least we can share information, resources, and linkages to the organizations. For example the Portland State University Research and Training Center on Family Support and Children's Mental Health (www.rtc.pdx.edu) supports conferences on such topics as building on family strengths, as well as an electronic forum section on the center's website for open discussion and inquiry. *Focal Points*, the Center's online magazine, is dedicated to families of youth with emotional disturbance. The University of South Florida Research and Training Center (http:// .rtckids.fmhi.usf.edu) focuses on how to improve services and outcomes for children with emotional disturbance and their families. It provides training, conferences and publications. Both centers welcome and support family member involvement in center activities. They continually seek input and feedback from families on everything from conferences, training, advocacy, research, and evaluation.

PARENT AND FAMILY EDUCATION

Over the last 20 years family education programs have been produced to address the families' concerns and to lend support. They are by far the easiest to implement, low budget, and manageable for most schools and community agencies. They are practical, accessible, frequently designed for specific groups, and widely available. School professionals that have worked to build strong relationships with parents and have made their schools family friendly, find these programs a logical extension of their efforts. Clearly, not every community can or will implement a family, school, and provider collaboration. However, parent and family education is a step that most schools and agencies can do.

What started as perfunctory information giving has developed into major initiatives aimed at both complementing and supporting ongoing special education efforts. The educational initiatives, largely focused on preventing problems, have yielded positive outcomes for students and their families and share the following five characteristics (Center for Substance Abuse Prevention, 1998).

- Focus on problem prevention rather than directly address existing problems (e.g. substance abuse, disruptive behavior) among children and adolescents.
- Focus on the dynamics of the family as a whole, not on one particular individual in the family.
- Based in theory that identifies the ways in which risks and protective factors interact to shape children's lives.
- Emphasize the importance of reducing risks factors and also increasing protective factors.
- Do not include parent education characterized by didactic, knowledge-only approaches.

Discussed below is a sample of educational programs and options. They include parenting children and adolescents with emotional disturbance and education programs to enhance family functioning, prevent behavior problems and promote mental health.

Educational programs focused on parenting children and adolescents with emotional disturbance address specific parenting issues and concerns. At the most fundamental level this includes any and all information given to parents as part of a student's initial special education assessment and screening as well as the ongoing individual education plan (IEP) process. For example in Pennsylvania the Department of Education, Bureau of Special Education provides a guidebook folder to start and maintain a home file of the student's special education involvement. It contains a resource listing including toll free telephone numbers. Specific educational materials are also available for parents of students with emotional disturbance. For example the Center for Effective Collaboration and Practice (www.cecp.air.org/) provides free and easily accessible two-or-three-page parenting tip sheets on several topics such as:

a. promoting resilience in children,
b. behavioral planning meetings,
c. self monitoring at home with your child,
d. direction instruction, and
e. universal preventative practices for use in the home for children with behavioral problems.

The tip sheets can be given to a parent to help with a specific issue or used as the basis of parent education workshops.

Education programs to enhance family functioning, prevent behavior problems and promote mental health have been developed with support from the U.S. Departments of Health and Human Services, Center for Substance Abuse Prevention (CSAP) (www.samhsa.gov/centers/csap/csap.html). Largely, the programs identified through these initiatives have an "academic" orientation with an emphasis on curricula, activities, and psycho-educational processes for specific populations. They are developed in universities through demonstration grants and research studies. The programs are frequently implemented by community agencies in collaboration with a school. Described below are a number of programs that focus on parents and might be considered as an offering by a school in collaboration with parents and community providers.

Linking the Interests of Families and Teachers (LIFT) is a research-based intervention program designed to prevent the development of aggressive and antisocial behavior in children within the elementary school setting. LIFT, developed by the Oregon Social Learning Center (www.oslc.org/), targets those child and parent behaviors thought to be most relevant to the development of adolescent delinquent and violent behaviors, namely child oppositional, defiant, and socially inept behavior and parent discipline and monitoring.

The Parent-Child Assistance Program (P-CAP) is a paraprofessional home visitation model for extremely high-risk substance abusing women. The program was developed at the University of Washington, School of Medicine (www.depts.washington.edu/fadu/) and uses a case-management approach. This is an effective complement to traditional substance abuse treatment, and focuses not simply on reducing alcohol and drug use, but on reducing other risk behaviors and addressing the health and social well-being of the mothers and their children. The program does not provide direct alcohol treatment, drug treatment, or clinical services, but instead offers consistent home visitation and links women and their families with a comprehensive array of existing community resources. Paraprofessional advocates have a maximum caseload of 15 families. They visit client homes, transport clients and their children to important appointments, link clients with appropriate service providers, and work actively within the context of the extended family.

Strengthening Hawaii Families (SHF) is a culturally relevant, family-focused prevention program designed by the Coalition for a Drug-Free Hawaii (CDFH) of Honolulu, Hawaii (www.drugfreehawaii.org). The program targets Pacific Island and Asian youth and their parents. SHF prevents substance abuse and related problems by improving family relationships and functioning, improving parenting skills, improving children's social skills, and by reducing behavioral problems among children. The SHF model provides the tools and process for elementary-school aged children and families to build on existing strengths through clarification of family and cultural values, family skills building, and nurturing connections among families, schools, and their communities. A standardized curriculum is used to deliver program content to groups of 6 to 10 families attending weekly 2-hour meetings. Through guided discussions, hands-on activities, and group sharing, SHF provides a framework within which families can discover what works best for them to improve family functioning and offers tools that can be used to strengthen family relationships.

Parenting Wisely (www.parentingwisely.com) intervention is a self-administered, computer-based program that teaches parents and their 9- to 18-year-old children important skills for combating risk factors for substance use and abuse. Parenting Wisely is aimed at families with delinquent children or children at risk for becoming delinquent or substance abusers. The program uses a risk-focused approach to reduce family conflict and child behavior problems, including stealing, vandalism, defiance of authority, bullying, and poor hygiene. The highly interactive and non-judgmental CD-ROM format accelerates learning, and parents use new skills immediately. The Parenting Wisely program reduces children's aggressive and disruptive behaviors, improves parenting skills, enhances family communication, develops mutual support, and increases parental supervision and appropriate discipline of their children.

Finally, school-based programs with strong family components have been developed to address specific needs of youth with emotional and behavioral needs. For example Project Safety Net addresses how schools can help youth with emotional disturbance complete their high school education and prepare for life after school (Ryan, 2001). Family involvement is a key project strategy.

CONCLUSION

Partnering and collaborating with families of students with an emotional disturbance for student and family success is a change from the traditional school family involvement strategies. The move to family centered approaches to meet the needs of students with an emotional disturbance and their families is only just now beginning to take hold. At the same time, we know that school collaborations and partnerships with families do not come about naturally or easily (Powell, 1998). Often there are struggles from the very first interactions between the school and families members. However, family members exert powerful influences over the development and adjustment of their children and adolescents. They are the key decision makers in the lives of students. Families and schools are partners and allies in helping children and adolescents with an emotional disturbance.

REFERENCES

Bickham, N., Pizarro, J., Warner, B., Rosenthal, B., & Weist, M. (1998). Family involvement in expanded school mental health. *Journal of School Health, 68*(10), 425-428.

Bryant–Comstock, S., Huff, B., & VanDenBerg, J. (1996). The evolution of the family advocacy movement. In B. Stroule (Ed.), *Children's mental health: Creating systems of care in a changing system.* Baltimore: Brooks Publishers.

Cheney, D., & Osher, T. (1997). Collaborate with families. *Journal of Emotional and Behavioral Disorders, 5*(1), 36-44, 54.

Center for Substance Abuse Prevention. (1998). *Preventing substance abuse among children and adolescents: Family-centered approaches, reference guide.* (DHHS Publication No. SMA 3223-FY98). Rockville, MD: Author.

DeChillo, N., Koren, P., & Mezera, M. (1996). Families and professionals in partnership. In B. Stroule (Ed.). *Children's mental health: Creating systems of care in a changing system.* Baltimore: Brooks Publishers.

Federation of Families for Children's Mental Health. (2001). *Blamed and ashamed.* Alexandria, VA: Author.

Federation of Families for Children's Mental Health. (1999). *Claiming Children: Special Theme Issue—Collaborating with Schools.* Alexandria, VA: Author.

Getzels, J. W. (1974). Socialization and education: A note on discontinuities. *Teachers College Record, 76*(2), 218-225.

Harry, B. (1992). *Cultural diversity, families and the special education system communication and empowerment.* New York: Teachers College Press.

Jordon, C., Orozco, E., & Averett, A. (2002). *Emerging Issues in School, Family, & Community Connections: Annual Synthesis, 2001.* Austin, TX: National Center for Family & Community Connections With Schools, Southwest Educational Development Laboratory.

Katz, L. G. (1984). *More talks with teachers.* Champaign, IL: ERIC Clearinghouse on Elementary and early Childhood Education (ERIC Document No. ED250099).

Kauffman, J. M., Lloyd, J. W., Baker, J., & Riedel, T. M. (1995). Inclusion of all students with emotional or behavioral disorders? Let's think again. *PhiDelta Kappan, 76,* 542-46.

Keyes, C. R. (2002). A way of thinking about parent/teacher partnerships for teachers. *International Journal of Early Years Education, 10*(3), 177-191.

Koren, P., & DeChillo, N. (1995). Empowering families whose children have emotional disorders. *Focal Point, 9,* 1–4.

Osher, T. W., & Osher, D. M. (2002). The paradigm shift to true collaboration with families. *Journal of Child and Family Studies, 11*(1), 47–60.

Osher, D. M., & Osher, T. W. (1995). Comprehensive and collaborative systems that work: A national agenda. In C. M. Nelson, R. Ruthrford, & B. I. Wolford (Eds.), *Developing comprehensive systems that work for troubled youth.* Richmond, KY: National Coalition for Juvenile Justice Services.

Powell, D. R. (1998). Reweaving parents into the fabric of early childhood education. *Young Children, 53*(5), 60–67. (ERIC document No. EJ570801).

Rogers, C. (1958). The characteristics of a helping relationship. *Personnel and Guidance Journal, 37*(1), 6–16.

Ryan, A. K. (2001). *Strengthening the safety net: How schools can help youth with emotional and behavioral needs complete their high school education and prepare for life after school.* Burlington, VT: School Research Office, University of Vermont.

Rumberger, R. W., & Larson, K. W. (1994). Keeping high-risk Chicano students in school: Lessons from a Los Angeles Middle School dropout prevention program. In R. J. Rossi (Ed.), *Schools and students at risk: Context and framework for positive change.* New York: Teachers College Press.

Simpson, J., Koroloff, N., Friesen, B., & Gac, J. (1999). Promising practices in family-provider collaboration. *Systems of care: Promising practices in children's mental health, 1998 Series, Vol. II.* Washington, DC: Center for Effective Collaboration and Practice, American Institute for Research.

Stroul, B. A., & Friedman, R. M. (1986). *A system of care for emotionally disturbed children & youth.* Washington, DC: National Institute of Mental Health.

US Department of Education. (1998). *Twentieth annual report to congress on the implementation of the Individuals with Disabilities Education Act.* Washington, DC: Author.

US Department of Education. (1994). *National agenda for achieving better results for children and youth with serious emotional disturbance.* Washington, DC: Author.

Wagner, M. (1995). Outcomes for youth with serious emotional disturbance in secondary school and early adulthood. *The future of children: Critical issues for children and youth, 5*(4), 90–112.

Woodruff, D., Osher, D., Hoffman, C., Gruner, A., King, M., Snow, S., & McIntire, J. (1999). *The Role of Education in a System of Care: Effectively serving children with emotional or behavioral disorders. Systems of Care: Promising Practices in Children's Mental Health, 1998 Series, Volume III.* Washington, DC: Center for Effective Collaboration and Practice, American Institute for Research.

Woodside, M., & McClam, T. (2002). *An introduction to human services* (4th Ed.). Pacific Grove, CA: Brooks/Cole.

Worthington, J., Hernandez, M., Friedman, B., & Uzzell, D. (2001). *Learning from Families: Identifying Service Strategies for Success. Systems of Care: Promising Practices in Children's Mental Health, 2001 Series, Volume II.* Washington, DC: Center for Effective Collaboration and Practice, American Institute for Research.

CHAPTER 7

TOWARD SUCCESSFUL COLLABORATION
Voices from Families of Children with Developmental Delays and Disabilities

Hwa Lee and Michaelene Ostrosky

Lindsay 's behavior is better than I had expected in the regular classroom. I thought she would have a difficult time. Her teachers have been very successful in getting Lindsay to perform activities, like wheel herself around the room or move her brush on paper at the easel, which she would never do for me at home. I thought she would be more passive and would refuse to try anything new. Her teachers report that Lindsay follows whatever is going on. She has learned the names of several children in the regular classroom and surprised Mrs. Hunt by greeting the kids by name.

Traditionally, parents of children with developmental disabilities were viewed as mere recipients of professional services. In addition, parents with

Promising Practices Connecting Schools to Families of Children with Special Needs, pages 101–127.
A Volume in: Family School Community Partnership Issues
Copyright © 2004 by Information Age Publishing, Inc.
All rights of reproduction in any form reserved.
ISBN: 1-930608-99-3 (hardcover), 1-930608-98-5 (paperback)

developmental disabilities were often blamed for their child's disabilities. This "parents-as-cause" perspective was associated with many types of disabilities such as mental retardation, autism, learning disabilities, and emotional disorders (Turnbull & Turnbull, 2001). For example, mothers of children with autism were once called "refrigerator mothers" indicating that they were too cold to their own children, thus causing the child's lack of attachment to their mothers (Maurice, 1994).

During the past two decades, however, the focus of educational practice for children with developmental disabilities and their families has shifted to a great extent, from a deficit model to a support model (Agosta & Melda, 1995). There has been a persistent attempt to include students with developmental disabilities into regular classrooms with their non-disabled peers and into the mainstream of community life (Agosta & Meida, 1995; Lesar, Trivette, & Dunst, 1995; Smith & Hilton, 1997; Winton, (1993). The process of inclusion into regular classrooms may be in conjunction with placement in a special day class, whose teacher serves as the primary lead of the child's educational activities both at school and with his or her family. The Individuals with Disabilities and Education Act (IDEA, 1997), also known as Public Law 105-17, and inclusive education efforts have provided many children with developmental disabilities access to equal education; however, for families of children with developmental disabilities to feel part of the mainstream the community, multi-faceted support and collaboration from school and community are critical (Lesar et al., 1995).

Among the 12 categories of disabilities created by IDEA, at least 5 are related to developmental disabilities. These include mental retardation, multiple disabilities, orthopedic impairments, autism, and traumatic brain injury. IDEA defines developmental disabilities as the following:

> A severe, chronic disability of a person 5 years of age or older, which is attributable to a mental or physical impairment or combination of mental and physical impairments; is manifested before the person attains age 22; is likely to continue indefinitely; results in substantial functional limitations in three or more areas of major life activity: 1) self-care, 2) receptive and expressive language, 3) learning, 4) mobility, 5) self-direction, and 6) economic self-sufficiency; and reflects the person's need for a combination and sequence of special, interdisciplinary, or generic care, treatment, or other services that are lifelong or of extended duration and are individually planned and coordinated.

In addition, IDEA provides a non-categorical classification term, *developmental delay*, used for young children between ages 3 through 9. Developmental delay generally refers to a delay in one or more of the developmental areas including cognitive, physical, adaptive, social/emotional, and language. IDEA suggests that this term also be used for infants and toddlers.

This chapter discusses the multiple aspects of challenges that families of children with developmental disabilities experience and discusses support strategies. Emphasis is given to family perspectives on the inclusion of their child into the educational setting and the community. Three sources of information included in this chapter are:

  a. research findings from the literature in the field of special education,
  b. quotes and interpretations from a case study involving three families of school-aged children with developmental disabilities, and
  c. interview and autobiographical data from a parent who has a young adult with a severe developmental disability.

The purpose of the family with young adult case study was to gain an understanding of families' experiences with their children's educational settings and other issues surrounding inclusion within and outside of school environments. All children whose parents participated in the case study had some type or combination of developmental disabilities, namely cerebral palsy, mental retardation, and autism. Each of these children was placed in some type of inclusive settings although the type and extent of inclusion varied. The families in the in-depth case study are fictitiously labeled Brown, Green, Rose, and Gray.

UNDERSTANDING FAMILIES OF CHILDREN WITH DEVELOPMENTAL DISABILITIES

Historically, individuals with disabilities were associated with negative social values, stigmatized, and cast into deviant roles in society (Goffman, 1963). Families of children with severe developmental disabilities may often experience such challenges as disrespect and prejudice toward their child, difficulty ensuring appropriate services for their child, long-term care, time constraints, mental and emotional health problems, and so forth. The more severe their child's disabilities are, the more severe their challenges will be. Most of these families are concerned with their child's independence and their child's future functioning as a productive citizen in society. Beginning in the 1930s, parents of children with developmental disabilities started to play active roles in their children's education. These roles include organization members, service developers, teachers, political advocates, educational decision makers, and collaborators. The roles that families assumed varied depending on their values, resources, and many other factors (Turnbull & Turnbull, 2001). Researchers and practitioners will agree that most parents who have children with developmental disabilities become an expert in the knowledge and intervention strategies

TABLE 1
Examples of Developmental Disabilities:
Characteristics, Etiology, and Prevalence*

Types of Disabilities	Characteristics	Prevalence
AUTISM/ASPERGER'S SYNDROME Unknown etiology.	• Impaired social interaction. • Difficulty with verbal & nonverbal communication. • Unusual or severely limited activities and interests. • May or may not have cognitive impairment. • Most individuals with Asperger's syndrome are of normal intelligence range.	2 to 10 in 10,000 people.
MENTAL RETARDATION Mental Retardation.	• Low intellectual functioning level. • Significant limitations in adaptive skills.	2.5 to 3 % of general population.
DOWN SYNDROME Extra genetic material from the 21# chromosome.	• Mental retardation. • Low muscle tone. • Heart problems. • Difficulty with speech.	1 in 1,000 live births.
GENETIC DISORDERS: PRADER-WILLI SYNDROME Lack of genes on one of the two chromosome 15s.	• A complex genetic disorder. • Mental retardation. • Learning disability. • Delayed physical development. • Low muscle tone. • Slow metabolism.	1 in 12,000 to 15,000.

FETAL ALCOHOL SYNDROME Maternal alcohol abuse during pregnancy.	• One of the leading causes of mental retardation. • Growth deficiencies. • Central nervous system dysfunction. • Craniofacial abnormalities. • Behavioral maladjustments.	1 out of every 750 live births.
CEREBRAL PALSY Damage to the brain where body movements and muscle coordination are controlled.	• Various types and severity. • Hyper or hypo muscle tone. • Mental retardation. • Seizures. • Hearing and/or vision problems.	500,000 individuals in the US. 1,200 to 1,500 preschool children with cerebral palsy are recognized yearly.

Notes: Sources are www.autism-society.org ,www.pwsausa.org, www.ucpa.org, www.nads.org, www.thearc.org, www.nads.org, www.nfxf.org.

related to their child's disability. Successful education for children with developmental disabilities should be based upon the collaboration between these parents and special educators who have appropriate training and enthusiasm (Lynch & Hanson, 1998; Romer & Umbreit, 1998; Winton, 2000). Table 1 presents characteristics, etiology, and prevalence of some developmental disabilities.

PARENTAL REACTION TO THE CHILD'S DISABILITY

Parents may display diverse reactions toward their child's disability. Factors such as socio-economic status, type and severity of their child's disability, cultural practices, values, and beliefs may influence their views of disability. While some parents may feel grief about their child's disability, others pursue pragmatic approaches immediately after their child's first diagnosis. Understanding the unique characteristics of each family is important for teachers and other school personnel. In addition, professionals should demonstrate appropriate sensitivity when sharing with parents information related to the child's disability. Parents of children with Down Syndrome, Fetal Alcohol Syndrome, and other types of developmental disabilities are faced with their child's disability immediately after their child's birth. It may be extremely hard for both the professionals and the parents to face the first diagnosis of the child's condition right after the child's birth. Cold and insensitive presentation of such information not only hurts family members' feelings but also negatively affects ongoing parent-professional collaboration as documented by case studies (Lynch & Hanson, 1998; Turnbull & Turnbull, 2001).

Professionals may also face challenges with families from diverse cultural backgrounds. Some families from diverse cultural groups may not always agree with their child's diagnosis and/or the types of services the families need. Some families may believe that they do not require services for their child with a disability or for themselves. Service providers on the other hand, may see a necessity for immediate intervention. Other families may be fully aware of their child's disability but choose to regard the disability as a private issue that should be dealt with by the family and not by an outside agency. A recent survey shows that while professionals generally agree with the importance of providing culturally appropriate services, they were not able to implement suggestions about how to do so, due to multiple barriers such as lack of funding, time constraints, lack of materials and resources, and lack of cultural awareness (Lee, Ostrosky, Bennett, & Fowler, 2003).

FAMILY-PROFESSIONAL PARTNERSHIP

Parents serve as the primary resource for teachers who seek to understand the student with developmental disabilities assigned to their classroom. As the caregivers and observers of the child since birth, parents possess a large depository of valuable information regarding the child's strengths and needs. This information should be tapped by teachers and incorporated into the child's educational plan. As indicated by numerous professional organizations, one of the most important qualities teachers and professionals should demonstrate is effective collaboration with parents (Association for Persons with Severe Handicaps, 1993; Division for Early Childhood, 1993; Smith & Hilton, 1997). A basis for teachers' work with any family is the knowledge of the impact a child's disability has on the family. Families often feel guilty for their lack of involvement in their child's education. Instead of blaming parents for lacking involvement, teachers support families and their children with developmental delays or disabilities by asking questions to understand parents' and children's concerns. Their responses to such queries will give the teacher knowledge on how to create an environment in which parents will feel comfortable enough to participate. Teachers should consider families' needs, aspirations, and resources as they collaborate with the parents on educational involvement. Some parents have too many obligations and stressors, so equal partnership with teachers may not be a realistic goal. In the following sections, voices from four families will be presented regarding their involvement in all three social systems, home, school, and community.

Parental Involvement: Home and school

During the entire transition to the new inclusive educational arrangement, all three sets of parents with school-aged children reported that they were actively involved in their children's education. The nature and the impact on each family, however, varied according to their resources, their beliefs, and the characteristics of the professionals who worked with their children. The Table 2 presents different types of family involvement by three families of children with developmental disabilities.

The Brown Family

Interviews with the Brown family provided the most active case of parent involvement among the three families. Their son was diagnosed with cerebral palsy and was mobile with the assistance of a wheelchair. Beginning with involving themselves in selecting the right teacher for their son Kyle,

TABLE 2
Types of Family Involvement

Setting	The Green Family	The Rose Family	The Brown Family
Transition Between Programs	• visited and observed six different programs • talked with teachers and principals • requested partially inclusive program	• contacted school personnel about future settings • discussion with teacher	• visited & observed future program • talked with principals & district personnel • prepared equipment for the classroom
Current School	• communication through phone and home-school notes • field trips	• transportation • communication with teachers and therapists	• prepared written IEP • weekly meeting • with inclusion team • daily visits • phone contacts • home-school notes
Home & Community	• physical therapy • transportation to clinics for therapies • story telling • the Green family activities	• home intervention facilitation • embedding behavior modification into daily life	• physical therapy • provide educational/ physical equipment • family activities (visits to parks, library, karate place)

the Brown family's involvement reaches to the extent that they are co-experts in their child's education in many aspects (see Table 2). Mrs. Brown describes her belief in parent involvement in the following excerpt:

> We feel very strongly that we are the main coordinators of our son's programs, not professionals. We need to have the education go the way we feel is right for our son and not have them direct. They should respect us at least as co-experts; someone who also has good ideas about the child. If the teacher does not want to communicate very well with parents, I don't think they are going to communicate well with the kids, either.

These parents not only feel that they are the main coordinators or co-experts in their child's educational program, they actually do as much, or more, than their child's teachers do. There are many steps that the Brown family routinely takes in planning for Kyle's education. First, each year before a new school year starts, Mrs. Brown observes several class-rooms of prospective teachers for the next school year. They then make a request to the principal regarding the qualifications they are looking for in Kyle's teacher, and they provide a rationale for these qualifications. The most important quality Kyle's parents seek in his teachers is a willingness to communicate with the parents and listen to the students. Once the setting is decided, Kyle's parents prepare for the IEP meeting. Throughout the school year they regularly involve themselves in weekly inclusion planning meetings in which the inclusion facilitator, teachers, and the teaching assistant participate.

The Brown family's involvement in the IEP planning and other meetings with teachers and school staff seems to be one of the most remarkable types of parent involvement. Before they participated in this year's IEP meeting, they planned and typed their own document containing information about Kyle's current abilities on the school IEP form. Their document was planned and organized so completely that it helped the teachers and support team gain a clear picture of Kyle's abilities and his special needs. The parent-designed IEP plan included not only the educational goals and objectives, but also sections such as Equipment and Adaptations, Inclusion Plan, Communication Between Team Members, and several checklists for daily activities. Mrs. Brown believes that parent participation in planning and writing the IEP report ahead of time will not only guarantee that parent requests are more likely to be honored, but also will be very helpful for professionals. This type of family involvement assists in establishing true parent-professional partnerships.

The Brown family reported that they are very satisfied with the way things have been going at school. In essence, they are satisfied because their expertise, opinions, and plans have been respected and implemented by school staff. This type of satisfaction stems from their full involvement in their child's school setting. Mrs. Brown expressed her opinion on this matter:

> When we were over at our son's previous setting, we were just amazed to see how many parents would say the program was really great and thought it was wonderful, and good for the child when they were never there. How do they know? How do you know it is going well if you aren't there observing how things are going? I think that the more information you can give them, the more involved you are, the more they will respect your opinions because if you are sitting back and just say "okay, yeah, that sounds good," then they are not as likely going to view you as someone with ideas and opinions.

Mrs. Brown does not mean that she involves herself to this degree because she does not trust professional integrity. Rather, as shown in the following excerpt, she thinks that active parent involvement can make professionals more informed, help them understand the child better, and guard them from taking their jobs too lightly:

I think that people are basically trying to do the best they can for the child. But if they have a parent actively pushing [for the child], I think that things are just bound to go further in the right directions because there are more people pushing [for the child]. If no one is pushing you for them, then it is easy to drop those things [for the child]. The therapy that they are getting in the first couple of years may lack important input and we felt that we really needed to be there to make sure that they were done. It is not that they are trying to do things badly but people are short on time and it is just the nature of people to do that.

Mrs. Brown indicated that some teachers and paraprofessionals may find this type of highly involved parents challenging, yet believes her involvement will better prepare the teachers. She even created several devices to help her son. For example, she created a floor chair for her son to sit at the same level with his peers during large group activities instead of remaining in the wheel chair.

For the Brown family, the most positive experience with professionals has been with their son's teaching assistant. Mrs. Brown especially appreciated the assistant's ability to communicate with her, to enthusiastically provide the support that Kyle needs, and to provide freedom for him to become more independent. The following quote from the Brown family, includes compliments about their child's teaching assistant:

> She is very confident in what she is doing and she is not afraid to take her own ideas and try things. She is very good at communicating with us parents, teachers, and therapists. She finds time to write notes for us daily. She pulls all of our concerns together and makes it work for Kyle. She is just really good. She also figured out what Kyle can do by himself. It is tempting to go up and do more for a child than what he needs. She has been really good at knowing when to step back. She is noticing that he is taking over a lot of things that she had been doing for him.

The Green Family

The Green family had fraternal twins, both with cerebral palsy plus other disabilities. Their son had mild cognitive impairment, was hyperactive, and demonstrated attention deficit disorder. The daughter demonstrated more severe symptoms of cerebral palsy and some visual impairment. Similar to the Brown family, the Green family had a very positive experience with their children's special education teacher. The supportive strategies identified by Mrs. Green were the teacher's ability to:

a. listen to the parents,
b. communicate with the parents on all matters, and
c. include the children in the regular classroom by collaborating with related school personnel and the parents.

Currently the Green family is very satisfied and grateful for their child's special education teacher. Mrs. Green shares the following thoughts:

> Mrs. Motts, the special education teacher is a very caring person. . . . It is not just a job that she is doing. Somehow, it is a mission if you want to put it that way. She also takes it in the right way with a lot of balance. And then, she respects the family. She asks for our opinions. She communicates a lot with us, very open communication. I think she is also very competent. She always comes up with new ideas. When something doesn't work, she looks for solutions, rather than wanting to label the child. So, she is pragmatic rather than wanting to fit the child into a category. She does not try to keep children in her room as much as possible, but rather she gives them tools that would help them function in the regular classroom. Maybe regular classroom teachers wouldn't be as cooperative if it had not been for Mrs. Motts.

As stated above, the Green family asserted that the teacher was very competent and a great supporter both as an inclusion facilitator and special education teacher. They believe that she respects parents and has been a great collaborator with other team members for their children's education. This educator will teach their children for two and a half more years, yet these parents are already worried about life after that. They think they are fortunate to have a teacher like her.

In addition to their children's special education teacher, the Green family also reported that community interagency support added to one child's positive adaptation to a public school classroom. They remarked their children's social worker in the previous setting often assisted in the transition process. The social worker helped the family not only during the transition process (e.g., making all the arrangements with six different settings) but she also helped their son in the preschool setting. When these parents expressed their concern about the need for their son to be toilet trained, his special education teacher told them that he was not quite ready. However, the social worker helped their son by taking him to the rest room frequently, which led to his becoming toilet trained. She also helped the family with their son's self-help skills by showing him a videotape of a boy dressing himself. The family was very grateful for her assistance because she took the time to try strategies that she felt might be helpful for her son.

The Rose Family

The Rose family was grateful to anyone that worked with their son. Their primary interest was for their autistic son to learn skills through one-on-one therapy. The Rose family valued the professionals' enthusiastic attitude as well as the ability to work with Sam and help him improve his speech and behavior. The parents are especially grateful to a woman who is enthusiastically working with their son daily for two hours. A substitute teacher, who is a mother of six children, teaches Sam pre-academic skills using songs, pictures, and other materials. The parents reported that she is very creative, and that her insights as a mother are her major strength. They feel lucky to have found someone like her.

As described above, parents in this study appreciated professionals who showed integrity and enthusiasm toward their children. These professionals included teachers as well as social workers, assistants, and other therapists who were helpful to their child and the family. What the families did not appreciate were professionals who were uncomfortable involving parents in the child's education and were reluctant to communicate with parents.

The Gray Family

The fourth family whose experiences are included in this chapter had a young adult son, Tom, with a physical developmental disability. Interviews with this family indicated that the mother's involvement in the child's education has been at the level of advocacy. The mother tried to increase public awareness toward individuals with severe disabilities. In addition to her duties at home with her son, she also communicated with local, state, and federal leaders for advocacy, gave presentations on disability awareness, actively participated in ensuring her son's right to be educated in regular classrooms, and arranged community volunteers for her son's social interaction.

According to these families, their involvement often resulted in securing the right program for their children, increasing parent-professional collaboration, and increasing the non-disabled children's awareness of disabilities. The Green family's involvement is one example of the effectiveness of parent involvement in their children's education. Maintaining equal partnerships between parents and professionals in all aspects of children's education is considered ideal (Dunst, Trivette, & Lapointe, 1992; Turnbull, Turnbull, & Blue-Banning, 1994; Winton, 2000).

The comprehensive positive type of family involvement that was described by the Brown family may not be possible for all parents who have children with developmental disabilities. However, creating a school environment where parent involvement is welcomed may facilitate this type of positive involvement. In order to do so, developing strategies to encourage and support parent involvement, especially for parents who have limited resources, should start with an examination of the types and nature of active parent involvement. Not all strategies that the Brown family used were time-consuming or labor-intensive. The type and degree of parent involvement may vary among families. Keeping the communication alive is the first step in encouraging parents to be involved in their child's education. An implication from the study is for professionals and parents to identify positive parental involvement strategies in order to develop a welcoming school environment. Also, future studies should focus on identifying barriers to parental involvement in inclusive settings. While the four families in this study believed that professionals do their best with every child, they indicated that parental involvement is both supporting and challenging.

Benefits and Concerns about Child's Setting

Each family evaluated their child's current placement in terms of his or her gains. Throughout the semester, all parents witnessed improvement in their children's behavior and/or skills. Although there are no data to support which, if any, of these gains were due to the effects of inclusion, parents reported that some gains were directly related to inclusion. Also, for all families, as concerns about inclusion lessened, new concerns about the current settings emerged. Some of the most significant benefits and concerns mentioned by the three families will be discussed in the following section. With the exception of the Brown family, who made daily visits to their child's school, the perceived benefits or concerns about inclusive settings were based on parents' communication with professionals and not on their actual observations of these settings.

Professional Support

Based on empowerment theory (Rappaport, 1981), Dunst et al. (1992) suggested a system of family-centered practices. They believe that families are capable of becoming competent if social systems do not fail to provide or create opportunities for competencies to be acquired. Parents expressed gratitude for the professional support they received. The type of support that parents described as beneficial and appreciated was the kind that was given voluntarily, the type that came from the bottom of professionals' hearts. Examples of this support included:

a.   a social worker who made six contacts with different schools and went with the family to all of the meetings;
b.   a special educator who enthusiastically helped a child become fully included;
c.   a teaching assistant who took her time to write daily notes about the details of a child's life at school;
d.   and two volunteers who, in addition to their work at school, took extra time and provided weekly baby-sitting for a family.

Parents were very grateful for these types of support. The implication for educators and researchers in the field of special education is to further

TABLE 3
Types of Support Professionals Provided to Facilitate Inclusion

Type of Support	Provider	Families		
		Green	Rose	Brown
arrangement of meetings/visits to future settings	social worker	✓		
home visits to discuss child progress	SE teacher	✓		
phone discussion	SE teacher	✓		
home-school notes	teacher assistant	✓	✓	✓
consulting parents for ideas	SE teacher IF	✓	✓	✓
disability awareness education for TDC	SE/RE teacher	✓		✓
teaching TDC strategies to interact with CD	SE teacher RE teacher	✓		✓
providing information about home intervention strategies	SE teacher	✓	✓	✓

Activity	Person			PT/OT
environmental arrangement	SE/RE teacher	✓		✓
providing solutions to behavior problems	SE teacher	✓	✓	✓
allowing CD room for independence	assistant		✓	✓
pull-out instructions for academic/adaptive skills	SE teacher	✓	✓	✓
including CD in all activities	RE teacher	✓		✓
	SE teacher			
establishing collaborative relationship with team members	team members	✓		✓
trying new ideas and strategies	SE/IF	✓		✓

Notes: CD: Children with Disabilities

IF: Inclusion Facilitator (A professional who provides services to enhance inclusion for children with disabilities in inclusive settings. Often, but not necessarily IF is the special education teacher.)

TDC: Typically Developing Children

RE: Regular Education

SE: special education

PT: Physical therapist

OT: occupational therapist

identify types of support that parents appreciate and how this support can be implemented in educational settings.

Studies of parent perceptions often present negative experiences with teachers and related professionals (Ryndak, Downing, Jacqueline, Morrison, & Williams, 1996). This family case study identified specific examples of positive strategies which teachers and school professionals can use to help children become better included in regular classrooms. Important strategies were:

a. frequent meetings with team members,
b. use of peers in instruction and other group activities,
c. arranging the classroom environment,
d. implementing new ideas, and
e. consulting with parents to solve problems.

These strategies should be carried out in a manner that fully involves parents in exchanging ideas, approving certain strategies, and being informed of the child's progress. Types of support families have perceived as positive are shown in Table 3.

THE MEANING OF SCHOOL INCLUSION FOR FAMILIES

Inclusion has both strong advocates and opponents (Fuchs & Fuchs, 1994). Many researchers and educators, however, consider inclusion to be effective based on their research and clinical experiences with parents and professionals (Guralnick, 1994; Peck, Carlson, & Helmstetter, 1992; Strain, 1990). In general, current studies support the findings of similar past studies on parental perceptions about the benefits of inclusion (Bailey & Winton, 1987; Bennett, Lee, & Leuke, 1996; Diamond & LeFurgy, 1994; Miller et al., 1992). Although all three families acknowledged the benefits of inclusion to some extent, not all of them considered fully inclusive settings appropriate for their children.

As the Green family involved themselves in inclusive settings, some of their perceptions changed while others remained unaltered. Their perceptions about how their children might behave in an inclusive setting changed due to their children's unexpected positive adjustment to that setting. In the following quote, Mrs. Green is surprised that after a couple of months her son was doing much better in the inclusive setting than she had expected:

> I thought he would do better in a quieter environment. But I think he really likes to be with more children. The teachers think what he likes is to be with other children and that might be a motivation for him. He is shy with them.

And he doesn't show his worst behaviors there. But somehow he is interested in what they are doing and occasionally he was playing with other children. He also is afraid of the regular classroom teacher. In the cross-categorical room, he gets too comfortable with the teacher and assistants. They are so caring and nice to him and he tests their limits.

This parent further shares how her two children with developmental disabilities are doing in their regular classroom:

One thing that surprised me is that my son's behavior is better than I had expected in the regular classroom. I thought he would have a harder time than he has had there. Teachers also have been very successful in getting my daughter to do some things, like wheel herself around the room or move her brush on paper at the easel which she would never do for me at home. I thought she would be more passive and would refuse to try anything new. They say Lindsay really seems interested in following whatever is going on. She also learned names of several children in the regular classroom and she surprised Mrs. Hunt by greeting the kids by name.

For this family, a more positive experience within the inclusive setting evolved over time, lessening the parents' concerns.

Mrs. Rose believed that her son with severe autistism would not benefit from fully inclusive settings until he learned appropriate social skills. The educators believed that the child should first learn pre-academic skills through behavioral techniques. Mrs. Rose stated:

Sam learns best in a one-on-one setting and we have teachers who come into our house and work with him on his own. If there is any sort of distraction, he just tunes out. So, when he is in a big group, he doesn't do well. I wish ideally, rather than being included in a big class, he could be in a class with about ten kids with similar problems, and they could be included for a certain portion of the day with normal kids. I'm not sure if I believe in full inclusion. I can't imagine him being in a regular classroom. Even with assistants, I think it would be chaotic.

Although the Rose family believes that a one-on-one setting is appropriate for their child, they hope that he will be included with mainstream classes for activities such as music, dance, and story time.

While the Rose family had trouble finding less inclusive setting for their child's education, Mrs. Gray shared the struggles she and her son faced to be included in the regular school. She wondered why children with special needs must fight for their right to be educated in regular school when it is a given for typically developing children.

It took 10 years for Tom to get included in regular education classrooms at school. "Mom, I no go back to Richmond School. I stay at U-High," begged

Tom, age 13, following a summer school experience at Richmond school for the disabled.

Using his liberator, Tom macros through these sentences:

My senior year in high school was the first time I was in all regular classes. I took Biology, Literature, Rhetoric, World Studies, U.S. History, Food and Nutrition, and Computer Literacy. There was no comparison to learning along side my peers. All the knowledge I had access to in those classes! Along with all the students I met, I graduated from the high school on June 2, 1992. As I went across the stage at my high school graduation, I unexpectedly received a long, warm ovation even though the principal had requested no applause until all 305 students had gone through the ceremony. The ovation occurred because I sat beside other students as a real class member.

The above emotional quotes indicate the difficulty this family went through to have their son included in regular school, and then the excitement they experienced when he graduated. However, they continued to experience obstacles. After a series of denials to equal educational access, Mrs. Gray got discouraged and stated:

How do you prepare someone who seems so vulnerable and at risk for a society that tends to degrade, devalue, discriminate? A question I ask myself every day. I seek academic inclusion: I demand it in a failing, overloaded school system. I feel discouraged and alone in this lifelong struggle for inclusive education for the child I give life to. "Is it worth it, Tom?" I query as I look at Tom. He glances at me, and without hesitation, nods his head yes.

As the three sets of parents with young children had more experience with their children's school settings, they began to experience the benefits of inclusion. In addition to the social and emotional benefits of having more friends available for interaction, some academic and behavioral gains also were reported. For example, Mrs. Green indicated that the main benefit for her daughter with multiple disabilities is social interaction, whereas her son, whose developmental disability was less severe, benefits both academically and socially from inclusive education. Although it is not clear whether these gains were the direct consequence of inclusive settings, parents strongly believe that these gains would not have occurred otherwise. This is similar to the findings of Miller et al. (1992) who found that participating parents believed that inclusive settings enhanced more positive child outcomes.

No matter how extensively a practice is advocated in the educational field, if the practice does not meet the needs and expectations of the family, it is not likely to be successful. Examining what type of inclusion works and under what conditions is a task for professionals in the field of special education. In order to accomplish this task, researchers must identify the diverse characteristics of each child with a disability and his or her family, the available program features, and the expected outcomes (Guralnick, 1997). In addition, as suggested by McLean and Hanline (1990), the traditional concept of least restrictive environment as a continuum of placements may need to be replaced by a concept of inclusive opportunities to be determined based on individual child and family needs, as well as community resources.

INCLUSION IN THE COMMUNITY

The issue of including children with disabilities and their families across all aspects of their lives has been addressed in a number of studies (Bennett, Lee, & Leuke, 1996; Lesar et al., 1995; Palmer, Fuller, Arora, & Nelson, 2001; Turnbull et al., 1994). Turnbull et al. (1994) claims that children with disabilities have the right to belong to families, neighborhoods, early childhood programs, and communities. In order to include children in natural settings, Turnbull and her colleagues suggest studying how children with disabilities develop a sense of belonging in various settings. Turnbull et al. (1994) generally conclude that parents had a broader definition of inclusion than has been described by professional organizations. For these parents, inclusion meant not only the child with a developmental disability but also other family members being included in all aspects of community life. Many parents were in favor of the educational services their children received in inclusive school settings, yet parents reported that they felt that inclusion ended at school. Parents also reported that their family life in the community was restricted and isolated due to the disability of their child. This issue of isolation is somewhat complex and difficult to interpret. Also, it is possible that the perceptions of these parents may have changed as their children got older. Further investigation into the expectations and needs of these families as they seek to be included in their communities is necessary. Additionally, research on the types of educational and social services that may enhance families' inclusion into diverse community settings will guide future efforts at supporting families of children with disabilities.

Family Involvement in the Community

All three families of young children with developmental disabilities in the case study stated that schools provided opportunities for their children with disabilities to interact with typically developing children. Once children leave school, how and in what ways were children included? Outside of school, all families were involved in their communities, but the types and degree of involvement varied among families. In the following quote Mrs. Green discussed the broader issue of community involvement:

> I think with this kind of child, unless the parents are very resourceful, and they push them, they want to try really to have them accepted by the community, by their neighbors no matter what. And without school, they would be very isolated.

Some parents, like the Greens, may have limited involvement in their community due to the restricted mobility of their children. Other parents may become involved in their community regardless of their child's disability by using resources available to them. The three families' interactions among family members, close relatives, neighbors, friends, and other community resources will be described in the following section. In the case of the fourth family, there was a pool of supportive individuals from the community who treated Tom sincerely:

> I integrate Tom in the community: We go to church, stores, restaurants, and the neighborhood. I ask for support from others: my husband helps some on a daily basis, while others tend to offer advice or a one-time assistance. Some evenings out without family and paid people are liberating. Relationships and membership in society are the real point. All interventions must serve that point. Keeping that point in focus provides an extraordinary challenge because it is a fundamentally different enterprise than designing a lesson or intervention. This relationship and membership building requires comfort with ambiguity, facility with perspective, and a storyteller's gifts for dialogue and plots.

The three families with younger children reported that their home provided many opportunities for their children with developmental disabilities to interact with their parents and siblings. All three families had more than one child and these parents valued interactions between siblings, including the child with a disability. It appeared that when a family had one or more siblings who were developing in a typical manner, the parents depended on them to provide opportunities for social interaction. This was especially true with the Rose family and may have contributed to their lessening concern over their child's social interaction skills at school. Extended family members such as grandparents or close relatives were not directly involved with the families studied; however, some extended family members did provide emotional support for these families.

All families utilized one or more community resources such as churches, libraries, parks, restaurants, or university facilities. For the Rose family, church is the major resource they use for their children's and their own socialization needs. All members of the family are very involved in their church, and with the four therapists who work with their son at home. Even on Sunday, one of the four therapists works with their son in a one-on-one situation while the rest of the family is at Sunday school. Two families were interested in summer programs offered by their park districts. However, after they received information about the programs, they were no longer interested because of the perceived lack of quality of services for children with disabilities.

Barriers to Community Involvement

Some families of children with developmental disabilities may have limited time to get involved in community activities. In some cases this may be due to the severity of a child's disability which demands a great deal of medical attention. At other times, it may be due to not enough time available after meeting their child's other needs (e.g., visits to doctors and therapists, home therapies, and the many other physical and emotional needs that these children require). The families who participated in this study reported that their interactions with neighborhood families were minimal. Also, some families were concerned about people's attitudes toward their children with disabilities.

The Green family reported the most concerns about community involvement. Mrs. Green discussed this concern in the following excerpt. This mother described her concerns about other people's attitudes toward her child in her wheelchair and she discussed general concerns about her child:

> Sometimes during our outings to the park, one child will approach us and ask about Lindsay. They ask why she is she sitting there, why she isn't walking, what had happened, and other kinds of questions related to a child in a wheelchair.
>
> Also, at a school conference, some would talk to me or ask about Tiffany, our typically developing daughter, but as Lindsay was reaching to them, as she sometimes does when we have conversations, they would just ignore her. Not even touch her hand or anything. I know very often she is covered with fluid. Other parents didn't mind touching her and try to interact with her and talk. I saw a problem not only for children but sometimes parents, very well-educated people in this community. Maybe they were not comfortable enough with a child with a difference. Maybe some parents have very high standards for their children. So, maybe they thought I would be uncomfortable having a child like that. I don't know how to interpret people's attitude but I see a big difference. Some parents are very nice. They really try to include her. Of course you can't include her in conversations but she reacts very positively, especially to female voices. She'll try to reach and she'll smile, and try to get out of her chair.

The above quotes represent examples of episodes that these families sometimes face. Parents reported that at the park, they usually do not mind answering other children's questions. However, they wished that these children were educated at home and school about children who have different needs. Also, in the second episode described above, Mrs. Green interpreted people's attitudes when they were exposed to her children. She reported that she felt comfortable when people approached her children and talked to them, rather than ignoring them or pretending that they hadn't noticed her children's disabilities.

As indicated in the following comments, the Green family reported that they occasionally get discouraged about getting involved in community activities, either because they do not have enough free time or because they are exhausted after meeting the needs of all their children. Mrs. Green explained these barriers:

> The big difference is the free time. We never take a vacation. We never travel except the one-day trip we made to St. Louis. And we never go to a restaurant or to fast food places with all the children because Lindsay will not eat and grows impatient. One of the neighbors invited us, but we are not going because we'll be very tired after this endless meeting tomorrow. And so, sometimes it is also our fault that we don't get social with other people. We know that it wouldn't be possible and it could be difficult. It is not just being embarrassed in front of other people, people we don't know, but it's mainly loss of energy.

In the case of the Rose family, the severity of their son's disability interferes with his social interaction skills. Mrs. Rose explained her reasons for not inviting friends over to play with her child:

> Two different times he was invited over to his friend's house, but he is just not interested in people at all. He just doesn't tune into people. Not just his friends of his age but anyone. For instance, my husband was out of town from Monday night through Wednesday night, and got back late on Wednesday night and didn't see Sam till breakfast time Thursday morning. And when my husband came into the room, Sam didn't even look at him. It was like he hadn't been gone. It has always been that way. He just doesn't show any reaction. I don't think he has any reaction. So, it seems kind of pointless to invite kids over to play with him. And then he is happy to see his teachers come. Sometimes he will respond spontaneously, and other times he'll just walk off that way.

The Brown family involved themselves in the community as much as possible. They take Kyle everywhere and try numerous activities with him, such as going to the park and library. Occasionally, Kyle visits his brother's martial arts class and observes him. Accessibility is an issue for this family as well as the Green family since both families have children in wheelchairs.

The Green family and the Brown family discussed their perceptions about several programs available in the community. They reported that these programs were not quite appropriate for children with disabilities.

For example, the Green family found that in one after school program run by the park district, some children with disabilities were neglected because there were not enough personnel to take care of all the children. In addition, the program lacked properly trained staff to meet the needs of children with disabilities. These two families find it especially hard to find summer activities for their children with disabilities when school is out. Although some schools provide a summer program for children with special needs, the program usually caters to children with disabilities and does not include all public school children. The Brown family, whose son does not have any cognitive delays, reported that they did not want to put their son in a summer program that contained children with cognitive delays and many different needs. Therefore, they keep him at home during the summer months.

Issues related to community involvement change as children with developmental disabilities grow up. The three sets of parents with young children expressed their concern regarding their child's future inclusion to society. The mother with an adult child addressed numerous obstacles that her child with a severe developmental disability had gone through. These obstacles included school personnel's attitudes from early childhood to post-secondary age, lack of respect toward her son, bureaucratic difficulties associated with access to services, and accessibility to adaptive devices. In the following quote, Mrs. Gray stated her frustrations with bureaucratic procedures:

> A letter of necessity must be written by an occupational therapist. A doctor must write a prescription. An insurance company must approve. If denied by the insurance company the first time, we must appeal. Tom may stand in his wheelchair again by summer. Or it may be Christmas. Tom must preserve the picture in his mind.
>
> Governmental and private agencies have mega bucks to administrate and study Tom, but not for direct services or equal status for Tom. The buck gets passed over, under, around, and through Tom, but never to Tom. And is paid support the ultimate goal anyway? I don't think so. Our experience has taught us money does not guarantee anything.

Individuals with severe developmental disabilities have limited access to services and events around them. However, due to recent technology advances in adaptive devices, more individuals enjoy independence. Mrs. Gray described the excitement over a new adaptive device that helped her son stand:

> Tom sat for 19 years. People talked down to Tom. People looked down at Tom. Expectations attached themselves to those downward talks and looks. Tom saw lots of midlines, halfway points. Occasionally, a person sat down beside Tom, talked to Tom, looked at Tom. Sometimes they couldn't stay too long; they found it extraordinarily complex to think and feel what it's like to be Tom on a daily basis.

> Today, Tom stands! He impatiently brushes Pat's hand away from the joy-stick; he's lived this moment in his mind an infinite number of times. Tom's the controller. Tom stands without me. My throat tightens, my chest con-stricts, my eyes tear. Tom talks face to face with Pat. Tom looks Pat directly in the eyes. Tom reluctantly returns to his cell of the non-standing chair.

Tom expressed his excitement over his first driving experience in a vehicle with assistive devices:

> When I'm going around town, I practice driving from the passenger side! One day, I plan to inform mom of my new position in the driver's seat. That'll add a few more gray hairs! As any young adult in college and working, but still living at home, I have taken over the car. So mom's cardiovascular system gets a great workout as she meanders through neighborhoods on foot, on her bike, or on the city bus.

CONCLUSION

All families introduced in this chapter shared their experiences of raising children with a developmental disability in the context of home, school, and the community. While they appreciated the educational practice of including children with developmental disabilities in regular classrooms, they also indicated they faced many challenges in all three settings. They also shared their struggles to ensure what they believe is the best for their child. They appeared to be involved in their communities as much as they could be, based on their time, energy, interests, and other resources. Edu-cators need to examine the nature of positive parent involvement and the types of support these parents receive from teachers, professionals, and community members. Not only should educators examine existing sup-ports, they should also develop and implement new, effective support plans for the families of children with developmental disabilities.

The community involvement of the four families in this chapter high-lights the social issues surrounding families of children with disabilities. Although participants in the study were involved in some community activ-ities similar to activities that families of typically developing children might encounter, there were barriers. Sometimes the barriers they faced were within the family, but most often they were related to a lack of school and community support. These barriers include physical and emotional demands from the responsibilities that come with children with disabili-ties. Other barriers are people's attitudes toward their children with dis-abilities, time, mobility, accessibility, lack of social support (e.g., respite care and summer programs), and the family's socialization style. One possi-ble interpretation regarding the family's community involvement is that these barriers made each family more cohesive. In these situations, family members depended on each other for major social interaction. Each participating family had multiple children, and siblings were seen as ideal social interaction partners for the child with a disability.

As the definition of inclusion broadens from school settings to community settings, educators should consider inclusion issues that occur outside of school. Future inclusive programs should strive to meet the needs of children with disabilities and their families in the community as well as the school. A discussion of who is responsible for inclusive practices outside the realm of school is beyond the scope of this paper. However, considering the current emphasis on viewing a child from an ecological perspective (Bronfenbrenner, 1979), and the emphasis on the family in the federal legislation, it is important to consider parent perceptions about inclusion within a broad social context. Professionals may need to cross professional boundaries and overcome bureaucratic limitations (Lesar et al., 1995). Future research should be expanded to include a richer array of valued social outcomes than studies have addressed to date.

For best results, services for children with disabilities should be provided by the school, parents, and the community, all working together.

REFERENCES

Agosta, J., & Melda, K. (1995). Supporting families who provide care at home for children with disabilities. *Exceptional Children, 62*(3), 271-182.

Association for Persons with Severe Handicaps. (1993, February). *Resolution on Inclusive Education*. Available from author, 29 W. Susquehanna Ave., Suite 210, Baltimore, MD 21204.

Bailey, D. B., & Winton, P. J. (1987). Stability and change in parents' expectations about mainstreaming. *Topics in Early Childhood Special Education, 7*(1), 61-72.

Bennett, T., Lee, H., & Leuke, B. (1996). Expectations and concerns: What mothers and fathers say about inclusion. *Education and Training in Mental Retardation and Developmental Disabilities, 33*(2), 108-122.

Bronfenbrenner, U. (1979). *The ecology of human development: Experiments by nature and design.* Cambridge, MA: Harvard University Press.

Diamond, K. E., & LeFurgy, W. G. (1994). Attitudes of parents of preschool children toward integration. *Early Education and Development, 5*(1), 69-77.

Division for Early Childhood. (1993). *Position statement on inclusion.* (Available from the Council for Exceptional Children, 2500 Baldwick Road, Suite 15, Pittsburgh, PA 15205).

Dunst, C. J., Trivette, C. M., & Lapointe, N. (1992). Toward clarification of the meaning and key elements of empowerment. *Family Science Review, 5*(1&2), 111-130.

Fuchs, D., & Fuchs, L. (1994). Inclusive education and the radicalization of special education reform. *Exceptional Children, 60,* 294-309.

Goffman, E. (1963). *Stigma: Notes on the management of spoiled identity.* Englewood Cliffs, NJ: Prentice-Hall.

Guralnick, M. (1994). Mothers' perceptions of the benefits and drawbacks of early benefits and drawbacks of early childhood mainstreaming. *Journal of Early Intervention, 18*(2), 168-183.

Guralnick, M. (1997). *The effectiveness of early intervention.* Baltimore: P.H. Brookes.

Individuals with Disabilities Education Act. (1997, March 12). *Assistance to States for the Education of Children with Disabilities and the Early Intervention Program for Infants and Toddlers with Disabilities.* 34 C.F.R., 300 & 303. Vol. 64, No. 48.

Lee, H., Ostrosky, M., Bennett, T., & Fowler, S. (2003). Perspectives of early intervention professionals about culturally appropriate practices. *Journal of Early Intervention, 25*(4), 281-295.

Lesar, S. H., Trivette, C. M., & Dunst, C. J. (1995). Families of children and adolescents with special needs across the life span. *Exceptional Children, 62*(3), 197-199.

Lynch, E. W., & Hanson, M. J. (1998). *Developing cross-cultural competence: A guide for working with children and their families.* Baltimore: Paul H. Brookes.

Maurice, C. (1994). *Let me hear your voice: A family's triumph over autism.* New York: Fawcett Books.

McLean, M., & Hanline, M. F. (1990). Providing early intervention services in integrated environments: Challenges and opportunities for the future. *Topics in Early Childhood Special Education, 10*(2), 62-77.

Miller, L. J., Strain, P. S., Boyd, K., Hunsicker, S., McKinley, J., & Wu, A. (1992). Parental attitudes toward integration. *Topics in Early Childhood Special Education, 12*(2), 230-246.

Palmer, D. S., Fuller, K., Arora, T., & Nelson, M. (2001). Taking sides: Parent views on inclusion for their children with severe disabilities. *Exceptional Children, 67*(4), 467-484.

Peck, C. A., Carlson, P., & Helmstetter, E. (1992). Parent and teacher perceptions of outcomes for typically developing children enrolled in integrated early childhood programs: A statewide survey. *Journal of Early Intervention, 16,* 53-63.

Rappaport, J. (1981). In praise of paradox: A social policy of empowerment over prevention. *American Journal of Community Psychology, 9,* 1-25.

Romer, E. F., & Umbreit, J. (1998). The effects of family-centered service coordination: A social validity study. *Journal of Early Intervention, 21*(2), 95-110.

Ryndak, D. L., Downing, J. E., Jacqueline, L. R., Morrison, A. P. , & Williams, L. J. (1996). Parents' perceptions of educational settings and services for children with moderate or severe disabilities. *Remedial and Special Education, 17*(2), 106-118.

Smith, J. D., & Hilton, A. (1997). The preparation and training of the educational community for the inclusion of students with developmental disabilities: The MRDD position. *Education and Training in Mental Retardation and Developmental Disabilities, 32*(1), 3-10.

Strain, P. S. (1990). LRE for preschool children with handicaps: What we know, what we should be doing. *Journal of Early Intervention, 14,* 291-296.

Turnbull, A. P., & Turnbull, H. R. (2001). *Families, professionals, and exceptionally: A special partnership* (pp. 2-19). New York: Merrill.

Turnbull, A. P., Turnbull, H. R., & Blue-Banning, M. (1994). Enhancing inclusion of infants and toddlers with disabilities and their families: A theoretical and programmatic analysis. *Infant Young Children, 7*(2), 1-14.

Winton, P. J. (1993). Providing family support in integrated settings: Research and recommendations. In C. A. Peck, S. L. Odom, & D. D. Bricker (Eds.), *Integrating young children with disabilities into community programs: Ecological perspectives on research and implementation* (pp. 65-80). Baltimore, MD: Paul H. Brookes.

Winton, P. J. (2000). Early childhood intervention personnel preparation: Backward mapping for future planning. *Topics in Early Childhood Special Education, 20*(2), 87–94.

CHAPTER 8

SCHOOL-FAMILY-COMMUNITY COLLABORATION FOR DEAF CHILDREN

Pat Hulsebosch and Lynda R. Myers

OVERVIEW OF EDUCATION FOR DEAF CHILDREN

Deaf Children in Society

Education is complex and takes place within a variety of contexts including home, school, community, and society (Bronfenbrenner, 1994). Education is most effective when people in those varying contexts communicate well with one another. Yet, because they are born into an auditory-focused world, communication is at the heart of the challenges faced by deaf children.

Deaf people, for much of history, have been seen as problematic (at best), or pathological (at worst). Deaf children were once thought of as hearing children who were broken (Spencer, Erting, & Marschark, 2000), and much of society still perceives deaf children to be disabled. During the last decade, perspectives on Deaf people have begun to shift from a medical model of "hearing impairment" to a cultural model of Deaf people with

Promising Practices Connecting Schools to Families of Children with Special Needs, pages 129–145.
A Volume in: Family School Community Partnership Issues
Copyright © 2004 by Information Age Publishing, Inc.
All rights of reproduction in any form reserved.
ISBN: 1-930608-99-3 (hardcover), 1-930608-98-5 (paperback)

a separate language (American Sign Language [ASL]), organizations (social, political, and athletic), and ways of knowing. Today many members of the Deaf community see themselves not as a people with a disability, but as members of a language minority whose native language is a signed language (Spencer et al., 2000).

More recent understandings of Deaf culture support an appreciation of the special qualities of deaf children, their commonalities with hearing children, as well as their unique ways of learning that require environmental adaptations. Deaf children eat, sleep, and play much like hearing children. But deaf[1] children take in information about the world (that is, they learn) visually. Thus, for deaf children, access to language and learning comes through the eyes rather than the ears. But most people—those who learn auditorily—do not easily understand the magnitude of this difference. As Jamieson notes, "It appears that hearing adults, both parents and teachers, face a tremendous challenge in trying to unlearn habitual communication patterns and to replace them with patterns more appropriate to the visual mode" (Spencer et al., 2000, p. 57).

Deaf Children and Their Families

Deaf parents are able to communicate with their Deaf children immediately, and "like the hearing child born to a well-functioning hearing family, the Deaf infant in a Deaf family . . . is immediately exposed to a world suited to maximizing his or her social, emotional, psychological, cognitive, and linguistic development" (Lane, Hoffmeister, & Bahan, 1996, p. 26). Deaf parents with deaf children bring to child-rearing years of implicit as well as explicit experience, knowledge, and attitudes about what it means to be Deaf. If the Deaf parents were born deaf, they have grown up responding visually to the world around them. Deaf parents intuitively think in visual ways, which is the best way to convey information to young deaf children who are just forming a language base (Erting, Prezioso, & O'Grady Hynes, 1994). Despite being reared in a society that sees them as disabled and seldom totally avoiding the attitudes of deficiency, Deaf parents know what they and their peers have been capable of, and are more attuned to the potential of deaf children.

Yet, most deaf children are not born to deaf parents. More than 90 percent of deaf children are born to hearing parents (Allen, 1986), the majority of whom have had no meaningful contact with Deaf people prior to the birth of their child. Hearing parents of deaf children thus spend the first few years of their child's life (and often beyond) attempting to understand what it means to be deaf and Deaf. They struggle with understanding what it means to be visually oriented in a world that is, itself, oriented toward sound. Hearing parents' first thoughts may be about their child's inability to hear music. They may later (or never) shift to a cultural perspective that allows them to think visually about day-to-day interactions. For example, with a visually-based cultural perspective, parents purposefully get their child's attention before attempting to communicate information. They also make a point of consciously informing their child where they are going before they leave the room. Subtle adaptations in how families go about doing things make a tremendous difference that allows the deaf child access to family activities and understandings.

Hearing parents' first experience of deafness usually comes when their child is "diagnosed" as deaf within the medical system. The focus on disability, the emphasis on the medical model of response, combined with their unfamiliarity with deafness, often results in families becoming uncertain about their abilities to parent their deaf child. As Scott and Dooley (1985) report, professionals "become viewed as more expert parents than the parents themselves" (p. 212). For hearing parents of deaf children, knowledge, processes, interactions, routines, and tasks about which parents would seldom think twice can become frustrating, and their normal parental capacities become frozen, or seemingly unavailable for use. One mother said, "I didn't know how to raise a deaf child. I felt guilty she had the burden of deafness and that she had been born to the wrong mother. I had never felt so helpless in my life" (Schwartz, 1996, p. 97). Hearing parents of deaf children may also share the dominant culture's norms and myths about deafness, which in turn influences their perceptions and expectations of their child. One parent stated "I had never met a deaf person in my life and I tried to imagine what kind of life deaf people led. Dark lonely images filled my head with questions that were too frightening to ponder. Can deaf people work? Can they be independent?" (Schwartz, 1996, p. 97). As a result of these feelings, deaf children may struggle for understanding, mirroring, and even typical parent-child interactions in their families.

Deaf Children and Schools

Moores (2001) contends that, since its inception, education of deaf children has been consumed by three basic questions:

a.   How should we teach deaf children?
b.   Where should we teach deaf children? and
c.   What should we teach deaf children?

A fourth question, "Who should teach deaf children?" might also be added to this list. Although these questions are not completely foreign to education for all children, they are particularly contentious in deaf education because of long-standing, heated controversies rooted in core differences in how those involved perceive deaf children (e.g., as disabled or as members of a cultural group) and the goals of their education (e.g., as enabling deaf children to be more like their hearing peers, or as based in a separate language and culture). Differing perspectives go hand-in-hand with differing educational decisions, such as those relating to the following options:

a.   ASL or oral English as a first language?
b.   Residential, mainstreamed cluster, or mainstreamed schooling?
c.   Home-based or school-based early education programs?
d.   Special education or general education curriculum?
e.   Hearing teachers or Deaf teachers?

Kirk, Gallaher, and Anastasiouw (2000) state that, "the education of the deaf is the most special of all areas of special education. . . . The special techniques that have been developed over the years to assist deaf children in processing information without the sense of hearing are certainly unique, ingenious, and highly specialized" (as cited in Moores, 2001, p. xi). On the other hand, some argue that the key to high quality education for deaf children lies in early direct access to a visual language, coupled with an understanding of Deaf culture. Wood (1988) argues that "the developmental and educational delays experienced by some deaf children may be the result of difficulties hearing parents and teachers have in making the necessary adaptations, or providing the scaffolding needed to help transmit knowledge and skills to the deaf child" (as cited in Spencer et al., 2000). Early access to native language (i.e., ASL) and Deaf cultural perspectives are a challenge since only about 15 percent of teachers of deaf children are themselves Deaf.

Educational options for deaf children and their families are varied. Options are inconsistently available depending upon locality and funding, and often conflict in philosophy and methodology. Although public education for deaf children typically begins between the ages of 3 and 6, the increasing occurrence of earlier identification of hearing loss means that families, as well as educators, struggle with a complicated maze of decision-making for deaf children from a very early age.

While all children are diverse, deaf children are additionally diverse depending on the age at which they become deaf, the amount (if any) of residual hearing they have, whether or not they have disabilities, their particular visual strengths and weaknesses, their family's reaction to learning of their deafness, and family cultural background. While educational options for deaf children are varied and variable, deaf children and their families also vary in the kinds of supports and services that may benefit them.

HOME-SCHOOL-COMMUNITY COLLABORATION

Benefits of Collaboration

Decades of research have shown the benefits of family involvement in the education of all children. Family involvement has been shown to have positive effects on student academic achievement, attendance, and more positive student and parent attitudes towards education (Henderson & Berla, 1994; U.S. Department of Education, 1994). Research on strong parent involvement programs has shown them to have the following characteristics:

a.   formal support (e.g., written policy, a coordinator, designated space);
b.   training for staff, parents, and community members;
c.   a partnership approach with two-way communication;
d.   networking to share information, resources, and expertise; and
e.   evaluation and continuous improvement processes (Williams & Chavkin, 1990).

The literature on parent involvement also describes its more problematic aspects, starting with varying definitions of what "involvement," "partnership," or "collaboration" means. Teachers, families, and community members may hold conflicting perceptions of their roles and the roles of other stakeholders. Historically, home-school-community relationships have most often been based in definitions and practices that are school-centered in that they focused on the values, priorities, and needs of schools (Southwest Educational Development Laboratory, 2002). Recent models of home-school involvement, especially in early education, describe family-centered models and practices (Hulsebosch & Logan, 1998; Roush & McWilliam, 1994). These practices emphasize support to families as an important goal, with families holding the power to make decisions on all aspects of school services. A family-centered model of collaboration focuses on the importance of understanding families' strengths, cultural approaches, and adaptive strategies, as well as their needs, in order to develop effective home-school-community relationships (Harry, 1996). Other theorists and practitioners emphasize models of home-school-community relationships that are reciprocal, in which knowledge between home and school (and sometimes community) is exchanged. Similarly, there is a balance of power among the partners, with each acknowledged as having strengths, knowledge, and needs (Delgado-Gaitan, 1990).

Collaboration in Deaf Education

While collaboration for the education of deaf children provides the same challenges and promises as in mainstream education, there are also unique aspects to school-family-community collaboration for deaf children. This collaboration in deaf education differs from general education in at least four ways:

a. the age at which education, and thus collaboration, typically begins for deaf children;
b. the conflicting emphases on "intervention" and family-centered models in the education of young deaf children and their families; and
c. the impact of recent understanding of Deaf people as a cultural and linguistic minority.

Early Identification and Education for Deaf Children

There is wide agreement that the more families know and understand about their child's education, and the more educators understand about families and their communities, the more effective will be education for the child. Collaborative partnerships between home, school, and community have been the means through which the members of these contexts learn from and about one another. For most children, these partnerships begin in kindergarten or preschool, when the child first participates in formal schooling. For deaf children, school-family-community collaborations are likely to begin early, as young as birth.

Early identification of hearing loss and family involvement in early education prior to 6 months of age have been shown to significantly increase the opportunities for deaf preschoolers to achieve age-appropriate developmental milestones (Yoghinaga-Itano & Apuzzo, 1998).

Newborn hearing loss is estimated to be twice that of all other screenable "disorders." Approximately 1 to 3 babies out of 1000 (1 to 3 in 100 in intensive care) will be born with permanent hearing loss. Currently the average age of identification of hearing loss is 14 months, but the American Academy of Pediatrics and other policy groups have set a goal that all children have their hearing assessed before the age of 3 months, with "early intervention" no later than 6 months. "Babies are born with the innate ability to acquire language. However, knowing if they can hear is crucial in determining how they acquire language" (Indiana Family and Social Services Administration, 2002).

Early Intervention Programs

From the moment a family learns that their child is deaf, they begin to wonder about what this will mean for their child and family constellation, and they begin to ask questions. There is a sense of urgency to these questions, particularly now, with our understanding of the significance of the earliest years—or even months—of life for learning. Language development and social interactions, two critical areas for growth and development, are the areas most often affected if deaf children do not have full access to a visual language from birth. Information and education for the families are usually the means for supporting this access for deaf children.

Because of the sense of urgency, these earliest home-school-community collaborations are often called early intervention programs. Yet that label comes with its own set of problems because the terminology itself reinforces the sense of pathology in the child and/or family. Furthermore, rather than setting a tone of collaborative partnership, early intervention implies the need for professionals to intervene in a situation (family-child interactions) that would otherwise be harmful. "In interactions with families, deafness is always the central focus . . . and children become 'the deaf-child' rather than a child who is deaf" (Scott & Dooley, 1985, p. 215). The family becomes a "family with a disability" that needs help from what Lane (1992) calls the "troubled persons industries" consisting of doctors, audiologists, speech therapists, and "educators of the deaf."

The Deaf Community

Educators know that learning, particularly for young children, begins in the home, ideally in a child's family. By learning about family patterns, beliefs, and values, educators can do a better job of supporting adaptive strategies that are already in place in the family (Harry, 1996). There has also been a great deal of documentation regarding the importance of culturally relevant pedagogy for all children, especially those from minority groups. Effective schools seek ways to create learning environments that fit with their cultural learning styles and act as both a mirror of the child's identity and experiences, as well as a window for all children into the experiences of others (McIntosh, & Style, 1988). Partnerships between home and school offer the possibility of bridging cultures. However, for deaf children it is not enough for only families and teachers to reach out to one another, especially if the families themselves are not members of the "Deaf world" (Lane et al., 1996). Connections among the adults in their immediate lives must be multiplied if a fuller cultural understanding is to be gained. With 85 percent of educators and 90 percent of parents hearing, connections to the Deaf community and culture are critically important for enhancing the knowledge, power, and efficacy of the families, as well as the schools of deaf children.

RECOMMENDED PARENT PRACTICES
IN DEAF EDUCATION

In deaf education an immediate universal need is for parents to have accurate information about their child's deafness and the program options available to the child.

For example, parents seek information about how to best communicate with their child and ways to encourage their child's development. Yet, their normal support networks do not have the experience parents are seeking, so early education programs can be the vehicles to provide families with support and information that encourages the families to aid their child's development (Bodner-Johnson & Sass-Lehrer, 1999).

However, with the tendency of professionals in deaf education to polarize around different perspectives (pathological vs. cultural) and educational theories, hearing parents are often left confused and unsure of how to advocate for their child. Most parents of deaf children have little personal experience or knowledge to use in deciding the many educational or developmental choices they are called upon to make (such as cochlear implants vs. hearing aids). Since parents must often rely on the judgments of professionals to treat or educate their deaf children at a very early age, they often experience uncertainty and loss of control over choices being made. As one parent commented,

> I think . . . when their child is first diagnosed you feel like all the control has been ripped out of your hands. Everything is now in someone else's hands and the most important thing seems to be to give some element of choice back to the parent and also to the children, so the parents feel like no one is treating them like a child (Schwartz, 1996, p.145).

Parental feelings of inadequacy are common, making it difficult for parents to be actively involved in schools (Calderon & Greenberg, 1997, p.143). Thus it is important that professionals working with parents of young deaf children be proactive in helping families identify their values, strengths, and resources to avoid de-skilling parents and relegating them to passive roles. New ideas about parent involvement recommend that professionals treat parents as equal members of the team, suggesting that programs adapt to the various needs of families by creating services that are flexible enough to meet individual situations, and responsive in ways that families find most helpful (Harry, 1996; Roush & McWilliam, 1994). The hope is that by empowering parents and supporting their knowledge of their own child, professionals can encourage/teach parents to become good advocates for their children (Sass-Lehrer, 2002). Similarly, members of the deaf community can provide important cultural insights and information, and they can be role models for families and children alike. There are four areas of parent/ community involvement in deaf education that we would like to suggest educators consider.

Connecting to the Deaf Community

Parents need a guide to help them enter into the Deaf community where they can gain access to cultural information, recourses, and services. They need help identifying which areas of the Deaf community are suitable for their family (i.e., churches/temples, Latino or African-American Deaf associations, political groups, sports groups, or Deaf clubs). We suggest that in addition to the school event information that newsletters typically provide, schools include information about Deaf community events, local Deaf peoples' accomplishments, and social services available in the community.

Mentoring

Parents can benefit from contact with Deaf adults or culturally aware hearing members of the deaf community (e.g., adults who grew up with deaf parents). This can be done via home visiting programs, parental tutoring, or community based Deaf-lead workshops. One home-based project is the Shared Reading Program sponsored by the Laurent Clerc National Deaf Education Center at Gallaudet University, in which Deaf adults visit hearing parents weekly with books in order to demonstrate how to support literacy for deaf children (Delk & Weidekamp, 1991).

Networking Structures

Since parents of deaf children report feeling isolated, there is a need to create opportunities for parents to come together to share, discuss, and advocate for their concerns. Helpful activities and methods to increase parental supports include the following: buddy systems (an experienced parent of a deaf child is paired with a new parent), in-school social activities, support groups, newsletters/list servers, and school reunions. Parents can also benefit from information that will allow their child access to the family's local community events, park district programs, and church events and programs. This might include information on the American with Disabilities Act (ADA), and local interpreter services.

Educational Structures

Parents need some skills to help them with their children's communication and developmental needs, be it sign language classes, cued speech training, or aural training. There is also a need for assistance dealing with the changing communication needs of the family as their child becomes older (e.g., behavior management, homework help, and dealing with dating and sexual education). The traditional backpack communication books traveling daily between home and school can be helpful for teachers sending home developmentally appropriate activities. Parents can then easily ask questions on a daily basis to gain information to help them build on their skills to bridge between home and school learning. Workshops for specific areas of concern, such as child safety, can be helpful for parents at different times across their child's development.

In the concluding section of this paper we will describe a community-based project whose aim was to establish (a) connections to the Deaf community, (b) mentoring, (c) networking structures for parents, and (d) opportunities for parent education among families of minority (Deaf) children, Deaf community members, and school personnel in a Deaf Education program. Through this depiction we shed light on the power of community-family-school relationships for the learning and development of deaf children.

THE DEAF PARENT-TO-PARENT PROJECT

The Deaf Parent-to-Parent Project (DPPP) was an initiative intended to bridge the cultural gaps between the Deaf community, hearing parents, and school personnel who are nurturing and educating deaf children. The goal was to provide structures within which Deaf parents who had raised Deaf children could share their indigenous knowledge about Deaf children with hearing parents through a series of workshops and subsequent mentoring relationships. The workshops hoped to provide the structure to initiate ongoing relationships, allowing Deaf parents to become resources and mentors to hearing parents raising deaf children, as well as to their schools. The Project's goals were as follows:

- To provide a rapid immersion in a cultural perspective on deafness that contrasts with the pathological perspective often encountered in the early years by hearing parents of deaf children;
- To increase the capacity of hearing parents of deaf children to respond to the developmental and socio-linguistic needs of their children;
- To tap into natural parenting capacities, supporting parents' self-confidence and accompanying abilities to advocate for their child within the school system; and
- To enable school personnel to better understand the strengths, needs, and experiences of both Deaf and hearing parents of deaf children.

When project staff set out to develop curriculum for the Deaf Parent-to-Parent Project, the goal was to join the growing body of research on indigenous knowledge in a minority community (in this case, the deaf community) with the experiences and mother wit, or native knowledge, of local Deaf parents. They had the following specific goals in mind:

- To support Deaf parents in articulating the things that they know intuitively about how deaf children think and learn;
- To identify techniques and concepts to promote perspective taking (from auditory/Hearing to visual/Deaf) in hearing parents raising deaf children;
- To organize and empower a core group of Deaf parent-leaders for workshops and mentoring relationships with hearing parents.

Although on the surface the Project's focus was on knowledge and skills for parents raising deaf children, the larger and deeper agenda was a broadening of worldview on what it means to raise a deaf child. Informal interactions among Deaf and hearing parents throughout the workshop conveyed many intangibles:

a. a realization that the Deaf can be independent and successful adults;
b. a belief in the significance of connections (bonding) between parent and child, even without a shared language;
c. a trust that their deaf children can continue to love them, even while becoming active members of the Deaf community.

The project began with six deaf parents of deaf children meeting in focus groups to brainstorm knowledge, strategies, and skills they knew from their own parenting experiences to be important in raising deaf children. When their discussions mirrored current research on best practice for deaf children, that research was provided to them to further validate the significance of their experiential and intuitive responses. These initial Deaf participants also formed the core of the project staff for workshops. Development sessions in preparation for our first workshops focused on strategies used by Deaf parents for optimizing the visual aspects of parent-child interactions. These techniques would be beneficial to all parents of deaf children regardless of the educational or communication choices that they have made. The strategies developed, based in a visual perspective, included the following:

- Visual-gestural play
- Using highly animated facial expressions
- Following the child's eye gaze to understand interest
- Moving into the child's line of sight rather than pointing
- Using touch to regain attention
- Reinterpreting the meaning of vigorous physical activity
- Visual presentation of early literacy

The final session established the format for the series of four two-hour parent workshops. The goal was to achieve a balance between time for informal interactions among Deaf mentors and hearing parents (and their children), and hands-on educational activities that could help hearing parents shift to a more visually oriented perspective. Families could then use these strategies at home and share them with other family members. Although the planning for workshops focused on parent-to-parent coaching and techniques for parent-child interactions, the Deaf parents knew their open and engaging involvement as mentors with hearing parents in Project activities was a critical part of the Project's curriculum.

With guidance from Deaf volunteers, project staff created goodie bags for workshop participants that provided resources that related to each workshop topic. Over the course of the four weeks, parents were provided with Deaf periodicals, specialty catalogs, Shared Reading bookmarks (Laurent Clerc National Deaf Education Center, n.d.), applications for loaner teletype phone devices for the deaf, forms for free membership in the American Society of Deaf Children with a sample newsletter, free rental information for captioned movies, state video library information, a description of Deaf sections at two public libraries, and pamphlets on the ADA law.

After the first year's workshops were held, we decided to have an annual community event, the Deaf Kids Fest, which was a held on a Sunday afternoon in a central location accessible by public transportation. Parents from all workshops and deaf volunteers were invited to meet to network and socialize. During the Deaf Kids Fest we introduced parents, volunteers, and Deaf community members to each other to increase networking possibilities for those in the same communities or schools. We provided visual entertainment geared to deaf children (signing balloon makers, deaf magicians, and clowns) to allow the whole family to enjoy Deaf culture. Exhibits from the local park district, TTY programs, and other local service providers were set up for parents to gather updated resource information for their families. This information was intended to link parents to the types of resources available in the Deaf community. We also sent newsletters at Thanksgiving and Easter/Passover providing information about Deaf community events such as Three Kings Day, Christmas, Purim parties, Deaf awareness days, and captioned movies in the Chicago area.

During the three years we offered a series of 20 workshops of four sessions each. About half of these workshops took place during the school day (usually first thing in the day to enable parents to attend a workshop prior to going to work). The other half of the workshops took place at night or on the weekend at sites connected with Deaf community organizations, including advocacy groups and churches. Most recruiting for groups was done through schools and early education programs.

The families who attended these workshops had deaf or hard-of-hearing children from birth to age 6. The families were 44 percent Latino, 32 percent African-American, 20 percent White, and 4 percent unspecified. Of these families, 24 percent of the parents were single mothers, 25 percent had only the deaf child in the home, 42 percent had two children, and 33 percent had three or more children in the home. Families included mothers, fathers, siblings (hearing and hard-of-hearing), grandparents, foster parents, and child-care providers. The majority of the families lived in urban Chicago.

Project workshops centered on education, in the broadest sense of the word, which can occur through communication and interaction. Through the project workshops we tried to create an environment where parents could reconnect with the pleasures of parenthood, learn new strategies, and understand the educational power of simple day-to-day interactions.

Workshops used a curriculum generated by Deaf parents, and were lead by Deaf professionals and Deaf parent volunteers. Deaf Project staff members communicated in American Sign Language (ASL), while hearing staff communicated in oral English. Interpreters translated ASL—and often Spanish, Arabic, or Chinese—into oral English. Children were present and took part in all activities, working alongside their parents. Parents saw volunteers enjoying and understanding their children while also witnessing and sharing their frustrations with their children. Siblings, extended family members, and, increasingly, school staff also attended sessions. An important part of the workshops was the parent-child interaction, then discussion of that interaction.

The workshops focused on depathologizing the deaf experience and reminding parents (and demonstrating to teachers) the parents' intuitive knowledge of children. Some of that occurred as Deaf adults described home lives that, in many ways, are like those of the hearing parents. Our volunteers were often asked if they can drive, if they were really married, how they could know their child is crying, and other basic questions about how deaf people live.

We also tried to help parents to better understand the realities that were different for their deaf child. We shared cultural/communication differences. For example, Deaf people naturally follow the line of eye gaze when trying to understand what a young deaf child wants, while hearing people tend to rely on the sounds and gestures that children make. Thus, when a child who has not yet developed a language is crying for something to eat, he points to the shelf and throws a tantrum. His or her hand is pointing and moving around while he becomes more upset. A deaf person tends to draw an invisible line from the child's eye to where he is looking, and then asks, while pointing, "Is this what you want?" This approach works well since children tend to get fixed on what they want and their eye is likely to remain on the item while the child's body is moving. The end result is that Deaf parents find the item sooner than hearing parents, with less frustration for both parties. We share communication hints like "watch the eyes" with the hearing parents to help them understand how to more easily attend to the communication needs of their child.

We also provided practical activities to promote comfortable and playful parent/child interaction that is not dependant on a shared language. In most workshops we played the *Copy Game*. This activity is like playing the drama game, *Mirror*, in which one person copies what the first person does. We asked parents to get down on the floor and copy whatever activity their child is doing. If the child is moving a car along the floor we asked parents to mimic the activity, keeping their face close to their child's, mirroring whatever facial expressions their child is making.

There are many purposes for this activity. First, it is non-verbal and non-judgmental, thus not frustrating for parent and child. Second, it helps parents learn how their child uses their eyes. There is a natural rhythm that deaf people use to shift eye gaze sequentially from activity to communication (Harris & Mohay, 1997). Since hearing people can talk and be involved in an activity simultaneously, most hearing parents are not in tune with that kind of sequential rhythm. Deaf parents help the hearing parents expand their use of facial expression during the activity to show them how the child will be more likely to maintain eye gaze if the parent is showing them interesting expressions. That improves the length of eye gazing behavior, which improves the opportunity to give the child information via visual communication (e.g., sign, gesture, cueing or lip-reading). Use of the copy game in the home allows the child to have control over an activity, which usually evolves into a game of *Follow the Leader*, which is very empowering for a deaf child. Over time the parents reported they saw a change in their child's self esteem and in their own understanding of timing in attempts to feed their child information.

We discuss techniques that can be used in the home and, after observing parental interaction, demonstrate adaptations that help parents become be more connected to and beneficial to their children, such as how to coordinate hands and eye movement while reading a book to a Deaf child. These techniques allowed parents to utilize their own parenting skills as they began to understand how to adapt to meet the conceptual and communication needs of their children.

Deaf parents can act as a catalyst for reawakening the intuitive knowledge of hearing parents raising deaf children. Seeing that other parents (Deaf and hearing) share common experiences, and seeing that simple parental interactions (such as playing the *Copy Game*) are an effective way to build and enjoy a relationship with their child, helps to reaffirm what parents already know.

A shared sense of social stigma also helps to unite parents of deaf children, allowing them to work together to challenge societal (and sometimes school) assumptions about the possibilities available to them and to their children. Deaf parents, as active leaders and family members, provide a reality check for both hearing parents and teachers about what the future can hold for deaf children. Deaf parents also serve as a bridge between the cultural knowledge of the Deaf community, the knowledge of educators, and parental knowledge and experiences. Thinking visually, following eye gaze, telling stories, and communicating by any means necessary are important reminders for all members of the home-school-community partnership.

Since we have begun working in the schools we have found that teachers are interested in learning more from the project team to further their own education. At one of the schools we had been working with for three years, parental involvement was identified as the deaf program's highest priority for staff development the next year. The program administrator marveled that this was the first time that topic had made the teachers' "top five" list.

NOTE

1.   In this paper we vary the capitalization of the first letter of the word "deaf." Beginning the word with a capital letter is typically used to signify people who participate in and identify with a Deaf cultural group. Uncapitalized use of the word deaf tends to be used more inclusively and typically describes people based on audiological status instead of participation in a cultural group.

REFERENCES

Allen, T. E. (1986). Patterns of academic achievement among hearing impaired students: 1974 and 1983. In A. N. Schildroth & M. A. Karchmer (Eds.), *Deaf children in America* (pp. 161-206). San Diego, CA: College Hill Press.

Bodner-Johnson, B., & Sass-Lehrer, M. (1999). *Family-school relationships: Concepts and premises*. Washington, DC: Pre-College National Mission Programs, Gallaudet University.

Bronfenbrenner, U. (1994). Ecological models of human development. In T. Husen & T. N. Postlethwaite (Eds.), *International encyclopedia of education* (2nd Ed., pp. 1643-1647). Oxford, UK: Pergamon Press/Elseiver Science.

Calderon, R., & Greenberg, M. (1997). The effectiveness of early intervention for deaf and hard of hearing children. In M. J. Guralnick (Ed.). *The effectiveness of early intervention: Directions for second generation research* (pp. 455-482). Baltimore: Paul Brookes.

Delgado-Gaitan, C. (1990). *Literacy for empowerment: The role of parents in children's education*. London: Falmer Press.

Delk, L., & Weidekamp, L. (1991). *Shared reading project: Evaluating implementation processes and family outcomes*. [Online] Retrieved 4/16/03 from http://clerc-center.gallaudet.edu/Products/Sharing-Results/sharedr eadingproject/

Erting, C. J., Prezioso, C., & O'Grady Hynes, M. (1994). The interactional context of deaf mother-infant communication. In V. Volterra & C. J. Erting (Eds.), *From gesture to language in hearing and deaf children* (pp. 97-106). Washington, DC: Gallaudet University Press.

Harris, M., & Mohay, H. (1997). Learning to look in the right place: A comparison of attentional behavior in deaf children with deaf and hearing mothers. *Journal of Deaf Studies and Deaf Education, 2*(2), 95-103.

Harry, B. (1996). Family literacy programs: Creating a fit with families of children with disabilities and family literacy: Directions in research and implications for practice. [Online] Retrieved January, 15, 2003, from www.ed.gov/pubs/famlit

Henderson, A., & Berla, N. (Eds.). (1994). *A new generation of evidence: The family is critical to student achievement*. Columbia, MD: National Committee for Citizens in Education.

Hulsebosch, P., & Logan, L. (1998). Breaking it up or breaking it down: Inner-city parents as co-constructors of school improvement. *Educational Horizons, 77*(1), 30-36.

Indiana Family and Social Services Administration. (2002, Spring). Newborn hearing screening: Early hearing loss identification can help babies communicate. *First Steps*. [Online] Retrieved March 27, 2003, from http://www.state.in.us/fssa/first_step/pubs/ magazine/page4.pdf

Kirk, S. A., Gallaher, J. J., & Anastasiouw, N. J. (2000). *Educating exceptional children*. (9th Ed.). Boston: Houghton Mifflin.

Lane, H. (1992). *The mask of benevolence: Disabling the Deaf community*. New York: Alfred Knopf.

Lane, H., Hoffmeister, R., & Bahan, B. (1996). *A Journey into the deaf-world*. San Diego, CA: DawnSign Press.

Laurent Clerc National Deaf Education Center. (n.d.). *The shared reading project*. [Online] Retrieved March 27, 2003, from http://clerccenter.gallaudet.edu/Literacy/srp/srp.html

McIntosh, P. & Style, E. (1988). Curriculum as window and mirror. (Monograph). *Listening for all voices: Balancing the school curriculum*. Summit, NY: Oak Knoll School.

Moores, D. F. (2001). *Educating the deaf: Psychology, principles, and practices* (5th Ed.). New York: Houghton Mifflin.

Roush, J., & McWilliam, R. A. (1994). Family-centered early intervention. In J. Roush & N. Matkin, (Eds.), *Infants and toddlers with hearing loss* (pp. 4-21). Timonium, MD: York.

Sass-Lehrer, M. (2002). *Early beginnings for families with deaf and hard of hearing children: Myths and facts of early intervention and guidelines for effective services.* Washington, DC: Larent Clerc National Deaf Education Center, Gallaudet University.

Schwartz, S. (1996). *Choices in deafness.* MD: Woodbine House.

Scott, S., & Dooley, D. (1985). Structural family therapy approach for treatment of deaf children. In D. Watson & G. Anderson (Eds.), *Counseling deaf people: Research and practice.* Little Rock, AR: Rehabilitation, Research, and Training Center.

Southwest Educational Development Laboratory. (2002). *Emerging issues in school, family, & community connections.* Austin, TX: National Center for Family & Community Connections with Schools.

Spencer, P., Erting, C., & Marschark, M. (Eds.). (2000). *The deaf child in the school and family.* Mahwah, NJ: Erlbaum Associates.

US Department of Education. (1994). *Strong families, strong schools: Building community partnerships for learning.* Washington, DC: Author.

Williams, D. L. & Chavkin, N. F. (1990). Essential elements of strong parent involvement programs. *Educational Leadership, 47,* 18-20.

Wood, A. J. (1988). Some effects of involving parents in the curriculum. *Trends in Education, 35,* 39-45.

Yoshinaga-Itano, C., & Apuzzo, M. (1998). Identification of hearing loss after 18 months is not early enough. *American Annals of the Deaf, 143,* 380-387.

CHAPTER 9

BRIDGING THE GAPS BETWEEN SCHOOLS, STUDENTS WITH PSYCHIATRIC ILLNESS AND . THEIR FAMILIES
A Hospital-Based Classroom

**Margie Buttignol, Shawna Lightbody,
Cheryl Williams, and Leigh Solomon**

This chapter describes a hospital-based school program operating out of the Child and Adolescent Mental Health Unit of North York General Hospital (NYGH) in Toronto, Canada. We highlight the importance of the hospital/education partnership in the care, treatment, and recovery of this highly vulnerable population of children and adolescents. The chapter is structured as follows: First, we explain the purpose for establishing this hospital-based school program. Next, the school program and the role of the teacher are described. We complete the chapter with challenges and a conclusion. Throughout, we emphasize the role of our hospital-based school program and the teacher in promoting well-being and a return to normalcy in children and adolescents requiring psychiatric hospitalization.

Promising Practices Connecting Schools to Families of Children with Special Needs, pages 147–155.
A Volume in: Family School Community Partnership Issues
Copyright © 2004 by Information Age Publishing, Inc.
All rights of reproduction in any form reserved.
ISBN: 1-930608-99-3 (hardcover), 1-930608-98-5 (paperback)

THE PURPOSE OF A HOSPITAL-BASED SCHOOL PROGRAM

The Ontario Ministry of Health (2003) recently allocated funding to develop specialized inpatient and transition support services for children and adolescents with mental health concerns. In response to the recognized need for intensive inpatient services, funds were allocated to regional pediatric hospitals across the greater Toronto area to create a network of inpatient psychiatric units. NYGH is one of the regional pediatric hospitals within the network that was allocated funding to open both inpatient and transitional services. The new Child and Adolescent Mental Health Unit opened in June 2001. The unit works as part of an integrated system of mental health services for children and youth. It collaborates with other network hospitals and with community-based services such as children's mental health agencies, child welfare agencies, and mainstream schools.

As part of our new unit, a hospital-based school program was developed. One critical community partner in this process has been the Ontario Ministry of Education (see http://www.edu.gov.on.ca/), which allocated funds for a full-time teacher through the Toronto Catholic District School Board (see http://www.tcdsb.org), Section 20 Programs. This classroom provides a therapeutic and academic milieu for inpatients and for those attending our day hospital. The classroom was designed to minimize the extent that hospitalized children fall behind in their studies, to normalize patients' experience while in hospital, and to help patients connect back to their own schools upon discharge.

Psychiatric illnesses have the potential to affect a child's success at school in a variety of ways. French and Tate (1998) discuss the impact of psychiatric conditions on both scholastic achievement and social functioning. The nature of certain psychiatric illnesses and the medications used to treat them can lead to temporary or permanent changes in cognitive functioning. In addition, psychiatric conditions may also be associated with deficits in social functioning, including poor peer relationships, refusal to participate in the classroom, and reluctance to attend school.

We know that poor school achievement (both academic and social) is associated with disability later in life (Kjelsberg, 1999). Therefore, school reintegration is a critical part of all individual treatment plans on the psychiatric unit. There is a strong recognition that without education, an individual's future employment prospects and ability to function within the community are threatened (Waltz, 2000). While patients with more severe mental illness tend to have poorer outcomes in these areas (Blanz & Schmidt, 2000; Pfeiffer & Strzelecki, 1990), it has been our experience that their participation in an academic program helps to promote a sense of accomplishment, competence, and hope for the future.

Although some inpatients are able to return to their schools immediately upon discharge from hospital, it has been our experience that other patients, particularly those who are recovering from a psychotic episode, require a more gradual reintegration into school. Some of our seriously ill patients have either not attended school, or have not been functional in their studies, for many months to a couple of years prior to hospitalization. In order to maintain the gains that are achieved during an inpatient stay and to minimize the risk of relapse, it is important to plan carefully for the transition back into the community. For these children and youth, transition to a day hospital program (also known as partial hospitalization) is an effective option, as it maintains a tight link with mental health supports while promoting greater independence.

It has been established that mental health treatment for children and adolescents should proceed in the least restrictive environment (Bickman, Foster, & Lambert, 1996; Blanz and Schmidt, 2000). Hospitalization is considered only when no other reasonable treatment options exist (Leon, Uziel-Miller, Lyons, & Tracy, 1999). When a hospitalization is required, the length of stay should be kept to a minimum to avoid disruption to a child or adolescent's life, always with the goal of reintegration back into the community as quickly as possible (Blanz & Schmidt, 2000; Gottlieb, Reid, Fortune, & Walters, 1990; Jaffa & Stott, 1999; Nurcombe, 1999). However, there is also a recognition that some patients, such as those with psychotic disorders, may require longer hospitalizations and may still show residual symptoms upon discharge (Borchardt & Garfinkel, 1991; Edell, Hoffman, Dipietro, & Harcherik, 1990; Lieberman, Wiitala, Elliott, McCromick, & Goyette, 1998).

THE CLASSROOM

As a therapeutic intervention, the classroom promotes a sense of competence, capitalizes on the child's strengths, and promotes well-being (French & Tate, 1998). Individualized support by the teacher ensures that expectations for each student are designed to promote success and build upon the strengths each student brings. Some students have told us the unit-based classroom provided them with their first positive educational experience in a long time, and gave them the confidence required to return to school.

At the NYGH child and adolescent unit, the majority of patients admitted to both inpatient and day programs present with risk of harm to self (i.e., self-injurious behavior, suicidal threats, or an actual suicide attempt) or have clinical presentations suggestive of a psychotic process. In fact, these two categories of presenting problems make up 70-90 percent of the reasons for admission. The other issues that lead to a child or adolescent being admitted to the unit include mood or anxiety problems that are impacting daily functioning, and individuals who are at risk of harm to others (i.e., homicidal ideation).

Individuals can be admitted to NYGH's child and adolescent inpatient unit or day hospital program up to their 19th birthday. Within the last year, the average age of individuals admitted to our program has been 15 years, with ages ranging from 7 to 18 years. Most of the children and adolescents who are admitted to our hospital unit have serious underlying psychiatric illnesses, such as mood or psychotic disorders. In addition, 10-20 percent have a comorbid autism spectrum disorder, developmental disability, or unusual medical syndrome that impacts their daily functioning.

While in our program, a treatment plan is developed, in collaboration with family members, to reduce the patient's symptomatology and to improve functioning across several domains. As mentioned above, one critical facet of the treatment plan is successful reintegration into school. In the first year we were open (September 2001-June 2002 academic year), 143 students were enrolled in our school program, with an average length of stay consisting of 14 days, or the equivalent of 3 school weeks. Some patients, primarily those recovering from a psychotic episode, attended the program for several months.

The classroom is situated on our inpatient unit, and both inpatient and day hospital patients attend the same school program. The school day runs from 9:00 a.m. to 3:00 p.m. Monday to Friday, and provides for a combination of academic and therapeutic work. While inpatient and day hospital patients were initially merged to accommodate space and staffing limitations, this model has proven to be valuable for both patients and staff. For patients, this merger has provided an unanticipated level of peer to peer support. For instance, viewing the progress patients who have moved from the inpatient unit to the day hospital program clearly encourages and supports inpatient peers. Those who are inpatients look forward to day hospital patients arriving for the school day. This integration helps to provide for some normalization of experience while in hospital. For staff, being involved with both inpatient and day hospital programs has allowed for improved continuity of patient care. It has also provided staff with a unique opportunity to play a role in the patient's recovery process throughout all phases of treatment on the unit.

THE ROLE OF THE TEACHER

On the child and adolescent unit the teacher is an integral part of the treatment team. A full-time teacher with expertise in special education plans the curriculum, interfaces with parents, and provides daily instruction. This teacher is supported in the classroom by registered nurses

(RN's) and Child & Youth Workers (CYW's). At the time of admission to either the inpatient unit or day hospital program, school consent forms are signed to allow the unit teacher to contact the student's previous school to obtain information from the student's Ontario Student Record file (OSR). The information is often helpful in formulating an accurate understanding of the patient situation. Specifically, this information helps us to determine whether there has been an acute change or chronic decline in the child's functioning prior to admission. It provides us with information about a child or adolescent's mental status based on narratives obtained from teachers, and it helps unit staff to obtain critical information about previous assessments and interventions.

The unit teacher conducts an academic screening at the time of admission for all patients admitted to the program, assessing decoding, reading comprehension, written language, and math. If a significant academic concern is identified, the team psychologist is consulted. This initial academic screening provides valuable information to the unit team about the child's current level of functioning. While this is beneficial to the psychiatrist in making a diagnosis, it is also helpful to the unit team for tailoring therapeutic activities to a level the patient can understand. It also serves as a baseline for monitoring changes in cognitive status and functioning.

At the time of discharge from the school program, the teacher plays a critical role in ensuring the child or adolescent's smooth transition back to the regular school. This often includes helping the teachers at the receiving school to develop an Individual Education Plan (IEP) that addresses program modification needs in relation to the identified illness. The teacher also acts as a resource to parents in their search for the most appropriate school setting for their child as some children, for various reasons, cannot return to their previous schools. The teacher also acts as a liaison and advocate for the receiving school in that she ensures that the unit treatment team has adequately addressed critical issues such as safety planning, education about psychiatric symptoms, and the impact the illness will have once the student returns to public school.

There is a strong recognition by the members of the child and adolescent unit treatment team that without the teacher's contributions, it is likely that many of our most seriously ill and at-risk children and youth would either not return to school or be sent into an education program not suited to their needs, thus threatening recovery. In fact, it has been stated that without educational programs on psychiatric units, the prognosis for a full recovery is diminished (French & Tate, 1998). In addition, without the assistance of the teacher, the onus of responsibility would fall upon family members or health care workers to negotiate with individual schools and boards of education. This is potentially problematic, as families and health care workers are not as familiar with the educational system and how to maneuver within it.

CHALLENGES

One of the biggest challenges we have faced on our unit is designing an academic program that meets the needs of a wide variety of patient situations. For instance, we serve patients with a wide range of ages, varied levels of intellectual functioning, and with various psychiatric diagnoses. Often, attention and concentration are impaired either due to illness or to side effects of medication. We have attempted to meet these challenges by having the unit teacher conduct an academic screening at the time of admission to estimate the patient's current level of functioning. This allows the teacher to modify activities and schoolwork to the patient's functional level. By having a CYW or RN in the classroom with the teacher, one to one support is available to patients who are having difficulty managing the classroom demands independently. Additional CYW and RN support is available for those unable to function in the classroom. Typically, patients admitted to our unit with major psychiatric disorders are unable to tolerate any participation in the classroom until an initial stabilization has occurred.

There are instances when particular patients have unique needs or characteristics that affect their ability to fit into the unit classroom milieu. For example, as described earlier, the unit primarily treats adolescents with major psychiatric disorders. A challenge arose when a 7-year-old male was admitted to hospital for making suicidal and homicidal threats, and for behaving in an unsafe way in a public school. Due to the preponderance of adolescent patients with major psychiatric conditions, the unit classroom was deemed to be an inappropriate milieu for this child. Instead, the teacher provided individual time with this boy when other staff were running therapeutic groups, and gave instructional material to CYW's to implement while she was teaching in the classroom with the older students.

Another example that reflects the difficulties of programming for a wide variety of patient situations occurred when a 17-year-old developmentally delayed male participated in the classroom current events group. In this group, patients are asked to read a section of the daily newspaper, and to complete a handout identifying relevant details and new information they have learned. Each patient is then asked to summarize his or her findings and new learning with the rest of the group. In fact, we have had many situations where patients with developmental disabilities participate in the same group as non-delayed children, and with students considered to be gifted. The teacher helps to pre-select newspaper passages that the developmentally disabled patients can read, often with some support from a staff member. She then provides multiple prompts to help these patients complete the exercise in a way that does not call attention to their struggles. When the patient presents his or her topic, the teacher may ask questions in a multiple-choice format to reduce pressure on the student. In addition, the nature of some psychiatric illnesses is such that patients can become "stuck" or overly preoccupied with certain topics. The unit teacher has become adept at identifying when this is likely to take place, and minimizes the chance of occurrence by editing material that could lead to distress or obsessive thinking, and redirecting patients off topics if they do become stuck. All of this is done in a subtle and sensitive manner, as patients are typically unaware of each other's diagnoses.

Another challenge has been accessing the most appropriate school environment into which the children and adolescents can transition after hospitalization. As mentioned earlier, in approximately 20 percent of our cases, patients have not been attending school at all, sometimes for a period of several years preceding hospital admission. It can be difficult to create any linkage to a public school when a child has been absent for a period of time. In these cases, the unit teacher locates the Ontario Students Record (OSR) when possible, and works to find an appropriate school placement. For example, the unit admitted a 15-year old boy who immigrated to Canada two years prior with his mother. He had enrolled in school but had only attended for about one month each of the two years. This boy had a developmental delay in addition to the major psychiatric illness that brought him to our unit. The unit team played an integral role in identifying the extent of his delay and in helping the family gain access to specialized support services, including a school-based day treatment program for developmentally delayed youth. This situation was particularly rewarding, as the young man had experienced intense anxiety about attending public school, and discovered through his hospital admission that he could make friends, achieve academically, and most importantly for him, he discovered that a teacher could be a supportive ally and role model.

For an additional example of a challenging transition, a 16-year-old male was admitted to the unit with psychosis. It became clear that this young man would not be able to function in a traditional classroom setting. His concentration was severely impaired, he required frequent breaks with emotional support from staff, and was prone to incidents of verbal aggression. In this case, the teacher helped to arrange a case conference with the patient, his family, team members, and representative(s) of the public school. The principal of the public school agreed that a traditional classroom arrangement was not a reasonable option, and worked with the board of education to get this young man enrolled in an alternative program. However, this new program was not able to accept him immediately. In the interim, the unit teacher worked with this patient in the day program to achieve a partial course credit while awaiting his alternative program. It is our experience that immediate solutions for appropriate academic placements are not always available. As a result, we work in conjunction with the community school to develop creative transition plans and longer-term solutions that are in the best interest of the patient and his or her family.

Finally, the mental health unit staff and teacher face a continued need to educate school personnel about psychiatric illness and the impact of illness on the child or adolescent's functioning. It has been our experience that there are many misconceptions and myths about mental illness. As a result, our unit team meets with public school personnel to provide inservice education about psychiatric illness, including symptoms of illness, treatment, and management of challenging behaviors. One example that highlights the need for this kind of education arose from a 15-year-old male who was brought to the hospital by police after a bizarre incident had occurred at the school. This young man turned over his desk, yelled strange comments at the teacher, and made verbal threats. Understandably, the teacher was concerned for her safety, and the school felt this behavior warranted police intervention. During the police interview, it became clear this young man required psychiatric assessment, as he was suspicious and fearful that others were attempting to hurt him. He was stabilized in our hospital, reported feeling embarrassed about the incident, and was concerned about the perceptions of others at school. In initial discussions with the school, the principal informed us of the plan for expulsion. However, after talking with the unit's treating team, the principal gained an understanding of the student's psychiatric condition and the context in which the aggressive incident occurred. He withdrew the expulsion plans.

CONCLUSION

One of the important variables in ensuring positive outcomes children and adolescents with mental health concerns is helping them to regain a sense of capability and success. The unit classroom is a critical part of this process. We know that success in the classroom dramatically increases the likelihood of success in the community, and we are only beginning to understand the longer-term impact this classroom experience has on patients' lives. To attest to the impact the teacher has, we regularly have patients return to the unit to see the teacher and to update her on their progress in their schools. In order to ensure the ongoing success of our program in treating this most vulnerable population, we continue to emphasize the value of the unit teacher and classroom to school personnel, the general public, as well as to health and education policy makers.

For more information about the Child and Adolescent Mental Health Unit of the North York General Hospital, contact Cheryl Williams, Coordinator/C.N.S. (North York General Hospital, 4001 Leslie Street, 7 North, Toronto, Ontario, M2K 1E1, Canada. Telephone: 416-756-6418, Fax: 416-756-6689; email: cwilliam@nygh.on.ca

REFERENCES

Bickman, L., Foster, M., & Lambert, W. (1996). Who gets hospitalized in a continuum of care? *Journal of the American Academy of Child and Adolescent Psychiatry, 35*(1), 74-80.

Blanz, B., & Schmidt, M. H. (2000). Preconditions and outcome of inpatient treatment in child and adolescent psychiatry. *Journal of Child Psychology and Psychiatry, 41*(6), 703-712.

Borchardt, C. M., & Garfinkel, B. D. (1991). Predictors of length of stay of psychiatric adolescent inpatients. *Journal of the American Academy of Child and Adolescent Psychiatry, 30*(6), 994-8.

Edell, W S., Hoffman, R. E., DiPietro, S. A., & Harcherik, D. F. (1990). Effects of long-term psychiatric hospitalization for young, treatment-refractory patients. *Hospital and Community Psychiatry, 41*(7), 780-785.

French, W., & Tate, A. (1998). Educational management. In J. Green & B. Jacobs (Eds.), *Inpatient Child Psychiatry: Modern Practice, Research and the Future*. Routledge: New York.

Gottlieb, S., Reid, S., Fortune, A., & Walters, D. (1990). Child/adolescent psychiatric inpatient admissions—Is the "least restrictive treatment" philosophy a reality? *Residential Treatment for Children & Youth, 7*(4), 29-39.

Jaffa, T., & Stott, C. (1999). Do inpatients on adolescent units recover? A study of outcome and acceptability of treatment. *European Child & Adolescent Psychiatry, 8*, 292-300.

Kjelsberg, E. (1999). A long-term follow-up study of adolescent psychiatric in-patients. Part III: Predictors of disability. *Acta Psychiatrica Scandinavica, 99*(4), 243-246.

Leon, S., Uziel-Miller, N., Lyons, J., & Tracy, P. (1999). Psychiatric hospitalization service utilization of children and adolescents in state custody. *Journal of the American Academy of Child & Adolescent Psychiatry, 38*(3), 305-310.

Lieberman, P. B., Wiitala, S. A., Elliott, B., McCormick, S., & Goyette, S. B. (1998). Decreasing length of stay: Are there effects on outcomes of psychiatric hospitalization? *American Journal of Psychiatry, 155*(7), 905-909

Nurcombe, B. (1999). Goal-directed treatment planning and the principles of brief hospitalization. *Journal of the American Academy of Child and Adolescent Psychiatry, 28*(1), 26-30.

Pfeiffer, S., & Strzelecki, S. (1990). Inpatient psychiatric treatment of children and adolescents: A review of outcome studies. *Journal of the American Academy of Child & Adolescent Psychiatry, 29*(6), 847-853.

Waltz, M. (2000). *Bipolar Disorders: A guide to helping children and adolescents*. Sebastopol, CA: O'Reilly & Associates.

Printed in the United States
15902LVS00005B/289-393

9 781930 608986